roses
REVEALED

good gardening

Secret O'Neill

DERMOT O'NEILL

roses

REVEALED

SPECIAL PHOTOGRAPHY BY SARAH CUTTLE

KYLE CATHIE LIMITED

PREVIOUS PAGE, LEFT: *Rosa* 'Blairii Number Two'
PREVIOUS PAGE, RIGHT: *Rosa* Gertrude Jekyll
RIGHT, TOP TO BOTTOM: *Rosa* 'Raubritter', *Rosa* Jacqueline du Pré, *Rosa* James Galway

DEDICATION

This book is dedicated to John and Wilma Cushnie whose continuing support means so much.

First published in Great Britain in 2006 by
Kyle Cathie Limited
122 Arlington Road
London NW1 7HP
general.enquiries@kyle-cathie.com
www.kylecathie.com

ISBN 1 85626 654 0
ISBN (13-digit) 978 1 85626 654 3

TEXT © 2006 Dermot O'Neill
DESIGN © 2006 Kyle Cathie Limited
PHOTOGRAPHS © 2006 Sarah Cuttle
See also other copyright acknowledgements on page 192

PROJECT EDITOR:	Jennifer Wheatley
DESIGNER:	Fran Rawlinson
COPY EDITOR:	Hilary Mandleburg
EDITORIAL ASSISTANT:	Vicki Murrell
SPECIAL PHOTOGRAPHY:	Sarah Cuttle (see also page 192)
PRODUCTION:	Sha Huxtable and Alice Holloway

Dermot O'Neill is hereby identified as the author of this work in accordance with Section 77 of the Copyright, Designs and Patents Act 1988.

A Cataloguing in Publication record for this title is available from the British Library.

Colour reproduction by Chromagraphics
Printed in Singapore by Tien-Wah Press

Contents

foreword

It has been a delight to read this book by Dermot O'Neill who, obviously, really appreciates his roses. The descriptions detail all their positive points in a most refreshing way and he suggests the best way to use them in the garden. However, at the same time, he does not flinch from describing any of their weak points too.

It is also refreshing to find a book that includes such a broad spectrum of varieties from the original wild species through the old roses of the nineteenth century and before to the most recent varieties. Most of the varieties are widely available but some are really quite rare and will be more of a challenge to track down. However the search itself can be very rewarding and indeed often leads one onto yet more delights and greater appreciation of the wonderfully diverse world of roses.

The roses selected in Part 1: Best Roses for Special Purposes – are very well chosen and will be extremely useful to those gardeners wanting suggestions for suitable varieties.

The cultural details are straightforward and have been drawn up by someone who must have planted many, many roses and has, in the process, discovered the best method.

Altogether this is a book I would thoroughly recommend to all gardeners who want to plant more roses in their garden.

DAVID AUSTIN

OPPOSITE: *Rosa* Charlotte

introduction

The sight of *Rosa* 'Albertine' in full flower is a memorable one. On a warm summer's day the sweet fragrance carries on the air, drifting through the garden. Seeing this rose in my garden is one of the reasons I grow roses – it's the combination of colour, scent and profusion of flower. It's part of the essence of summer and it's what transforms a garden into a place of magic and atmosphere.

My grandmother grew many old-fashioned roses and I recall many hours as a boy in her garden surrounded by such wonderful roses as 'Madame Isaac Pereire', whose fragrance reminded me of a bowl of freshly picked raspberries. There was 'William Lobb', whose colour changed from purple through to violet and plum. Then there was 'Cardinal de Richelieu', whose velvet petals looked as if they were cut from the same rich fabric that Cardinal de Richelieu wore.

LEFT: *Rosa* 'Albertine'   ABOVE: *Rosa* 'William Lobb'

I also recall a sumptuous, blood-red climbing rose called 'Guinée'. My grandmother always referred to it as a greedy plant and each year I remember it getting buckets of well-rotted farmyard manure. The results of this cosseting were large, deepest-red blooms, which opened from almost black buds to produce the quintessential romantic rose. Powerfully scented, this rose made a statement, declaring its presence to all who came close. As a result of seeing my grandmother's roses and how she cared for them, I realised early on that roses had the power to cast a spell over everybody who came in contact with them. They create enduring memories, transform our gardens and, most of all, add beauty to the world we live in.

My journey discovering roses has brought me to many gardens and has introduced me to many people, including the late Graham Stuart Thomas, who was responsible for popularising old-fashioned roses and also for saving many old varieties from extinction. I recall spending a day with him and being fascinated and enthralled by his depth of knowledge. I came away enthused after our meeting, simply wanting to grow as many good roses as possible. A favourite rose of his was 'Reine des Violettes', which I in turn grew to love.

Other great gardeners have also played a role in influencing the roses I grow. The late John Conan encouraged me to grow many fabulous old-fashioned roses, such as 'Mermaid'. I look at them today and remember his encouraging words that started me off on this adventure.

While still at school, I worked part-time at Marlfield, a famous garden centre and nursery south of Dublin. It was owned by Ireland's best-loved television gardener of the day, Barney Johnson. The experience of working there has given me many memories that I still cherish today. Seeing roses being grown on a large nursery scale and watching expert nurserymen, who had spent a lifetime practising their craft, was a revelation. I can recall watching roses being budded (grafted) and being fascinated by the process.

It was at Marlfield that I first met Sean McCann, regarded by many as Ireland's foremost rose authority. Sean encouraged me to look at roses in a different way. I was fascinated by his breeding programme and the way in which he developed new roses. Sean's practical, down-to-earth approach gave me all the information I needed to grow roses easily and without complication when I was starting off on my own.

Since those early days I'm glad to say that I have made so many friends, all of whom share my passion for growing these wonderful plants. Today in Ireland there are great rose growers, like Brian Hughes, and rose breeders, like David Kenny, all of whom are contributing to the Irish rose legacy. It's nice to know that Ireland is playing its part in a small way on the international rose stage. I'm still a believer, though, in looking outwards at what others are doing and in the course of my travels to gardens around the world, it's always the roses that catch my eye. I'm particularly thrilled when I see David Austin's roses, which I grow in my own garden, flourishing in other gardens, be it in South Africa, France or the United Kingdom.

The roses featured in this book are my personal choice. All have what I call the 'X factor' – that intangible quality which sets them apart from other roses. They all have many of the essential characteristics people want from a rose. Each one offers the grower value for money, as well as having a combination of exceptional qualities. I have included roses known for their exquisite scent, their long flowering period or their disease-resistance. They are all roses that go the extra mile in providing the gardener with as much value as possible for the

Rosa 'Comte de Chambord' takes centre stage at Le Jardin des Rosiers in La Puye, France

space they occupy in a garden. Each rose has been chosen because it stands out from the crowd and has that special edge over other varieties.

Roses Revealed is organised in an easy-to-follow format, making it possible for you to select the rose best suited to a particular purpose. For example, if you're trying to find a rose that will make an ideal hedge, or if you're looking for one that has exceptionally good fragrance, or if you're simply looking for the very best red rose, this book makes it easy in that the work is already done for you. These 'best' roses are included in Part 1: Best Roses for Special Purposes. Part 2: Directory of Roses is laid out so that you can easily find a rose, firstly by its type, be it a climber, shrub or bush rose. The roses within each type are then subdivided by colour, so if you're looking for a particular shade, it's easy to reference

your choice. Finally, Part 3: Rose Care is just what it says – a highly practical rose-care section presented in a simple, no-frills way, which gives you the information you need to always get the best from your roses. In addition, the Rose Finder at the back lists all the roses and their uses so you can find at a glance what you are looking for.

No other flower has permeated our collective subconscious in the same way as the rose. It has been reported by psychologists that the first flower people think of when asked is a red rose – which only goes to prove that the rose is the flower of flowers, not only in our gardens but in our imaginations too. I believe that the selection in this book reflects the best of the best.

DERMOT O'NEILL

BEST

roses

FOR SPECIAL

PURPOSES

best scented roses

I found it difficult to select my favourite scented roses. There
are dozens of really good ones, but here are a few of my personal
favourites which add superb fragrance to any garden.

Fragrant Cloud

If ever a rose lived up to its name,
it is Fragrant Cloud. Bred in the
1960s, today it is regarded as a
great classic. My mother and
grandmother both grew it, and I
can remember it from my
childhood. Only recently I came
across it again. The moment I
inhaled its sweet fragrance I was
transported back in time. It's
amazing how powerful a reminder a
fragrance can be. The scent was so
magical, I decided there and then
that this was a 'must-have' rose that
I hope I'll never again be without.
Since its introduction, Fragrant
Cloud has continued to win top
rose awards all over the world
including, in 1970, the Alexander
Gamble Rose Fragrance Award and,
in 1981, the World's Favourite Rose
Award, as chosen by popular vote
in the member countries of the
World Federation of Rose Societies
and announced at World Rose
Conventions. These awards are
testimony to its continuing
popularity. The flowers are an
unusual vermilion-red colour.

DIRECTORY p133

Papa Meilland

Papa Meilland is all a rose should be and is regarded by many leading experts as the world's greatest crimson rose. It has to be one of the most sumptuous roses you can grow. You may wonder why it's not in our 'Best Red Rose' section, well, let me tell you it also has a powerful fragrance – opulent, penetrating and sweet – to match the richness of its colour. The buds are exquisitely and perfectly pointed and the flowers open to velvet crimson blooms with recurved petals. These flowers are very large and always appear one per stem, which makes them perfect as cut flowers. I've tried growing Papa Meilland in Ireland, but it prefers warmer conditions, so I've thought of growing it in a conservatory. That would give it the protection it needs and shelter from our wet winters, but the main reason for having it in a conservatory would be to capture its penetrating, sugary sweet fragrance and be able to enjoy it at close quarters.

DIRECTORY p133

Sénégal

This climbing rose is not widely available but it's worth seeking it out. I understand that it can be ordered from Peter Beales' back catalogue and from Roseraie de Berty in France (see Resources, page 184). Its fragrance is above and beyond that of many roses and reminds me of opening a box of rose-flavoured Turkish delight on Christmas morning – a delicious fruity perfume, rich and intoxicating, powerful, heady and sweet. I first bought 'Sénégal' from a nursery in the south of France and have now grown it on a low fence for many years. It flowers here throughout the summer, giving an especially good flush in June. It's one of the deepest red Climbing roses I grow, with blossoms of a deep purple-red, the colour of a great Bordeaux wine. As the buds open, the colour brings to mind the richness of purple plums covered in powdery bloom. There's a moment every year when I find myself falling in love with 'Sénégal' all over again and it's just as the first flowers begin to open and the new growth is still fresh. Then the leaves are the colour of stewed rhubarb and when the sunlight catches them they glow. DIRECTORY p159

Souvenir du Docteur Jamain

This wonderful old climbing rose was a great favourite of the writer and gardener Vita Sackville-West who is famous for her garden at Sissinghurst in Kent. It's a rose you'll always find in the very best of gardens, but it's not one I would recommend for a beginner. However, treat it like a prima donna and it will reward you with an exceptional performance – a display of incomparable, darkly rich, velvet-textured wine-red roses which, in some lights, verge on black. Their scent is strong, sweet and complex. I sometimes detect spicy notes blended with vanilla. But fail to look after this rose and it will sulk and not produce flowers at all. I saw a great example of it growing at Jim Reynold's rose garden in Butterstream, Trim, Co. Meath. It was grown on the shaded side of a grey stone wall, the colour of which made the flowers stand out like rubies. It trailed over an archway leading from one part of the garden to another. I remember thinking what a super choice of position this was, as every visitor was able to have a close encounter with its blossoms and enthralling scent as they walked through the garden. DIRECTORY p159

Madame Isaac Pereire

Bourbon roses rank among the most richly fragrant of all roses and the opulent 'Madame Isaac Pereire' stands out from this select crowd as being exceptionally beautiful in every way. Developed in France in 1881 and named after a member of a prominent banking family, it really has stood the test of time; I think this 'to die for' rose should be in every old-rose collector's garden. It is everything an old rose should be. The double, deep pink to magenta flowers are an example of full-petalled perfection – enormous and cup-shaped. The colour is a deep pink with a feint veil of clouded magenta embracing each flower. I can only describe its fragrance as exquisitely sumptuous, reminiscent of a bowl of freshly picked sweet raspberries and nectarines with hints of spice. Like many old roses it gives its first flush in June and this is often followed in autumn by an even better display. DIRECTORY p151

Rhapsody in Blue

This award-winning rose created great excitement when it took centre stage in the rose world. Hailed as the first near-blue rose, it certainly captured the collective imagination and was voted Rose of the Year in 2003 by global panels of experts. On top of this, Rhapsody in Blue has received numerous awards for its exceptional fragrance – fruit notes of peach, lemon and honey come to mind. I wasn't sure I'd like a blue rose but, on my first encounter with it, I wasn't disappointed. Its colour is extremely pleasing and easy to use in the garden and I imagine it's a flower arranger's delight as it's so different to all the other roses we grow. Renowned plantswoman Helen Dillon grows it to visual perfection in her Dublin garden, combining it with *Salvia verticillata* 'Purple Rain'. To sum up, I think it's fair to say that this isn't just a novelty rose, but is one that's quickly establishing itself as a first-class garden plant – definitely a plant with the 'X factor'. I recommend you try it.

DIRECTORY p143

best red roses

When I ask anyone to think of a flower, the first that usually jumps
to their mind is a red rose. The red rose is associated with romance
and is one of the most beautiful of our garden plants. Here is a
selection of some of my favourites.

Dortmund

The wooden gates to my walled garden
are painted a vivid Oriental red. They're
roughly two and a half metres wide by
two and a half metres high and are very
eye-catching. I have planted *Ceanothus
arboreus* 'Trewithen Blue' each side of
the gateway. Its glossy green foliage acts
as a vivid contrast to the red. I was
anxious to plant a red-flowering
climbing rose nearby to pick up the
red of the gates, and that's when I came
across 'Dortmund'. It's fantastic. I have
it against the wall where it grows
approximately two metres tall and its
flowers complement my gates to
perfection, exactly as I intended.
'Dortmund' is also very effective in
front of a dark green background. I've
recently planted some in front of a yew
hedge and the contrast is striking. I'm
also very impressed with the habit of the
plant which, with a little training, is neat
and tidy. But it's the flowers that are so
special. They are large and single.
Brilliant cherry-red is probably the best
way to describe the colour. The centre
of each is white and the purity of this
splash of contrast gives a vibrancy to
the flower. DIRECTORY p158

Empereur du Maroc

I've always had a fascination with the darkest red roses and it's hard to find one with flowers as dark as those of 'Empereur du Maroc'. Before they open, the buds are truly black, and when in full flower the texture of the petals is like velvet. This is a rose that's so red it's exceptional, but it needs careful positioning to show off its colour. A light-coloured background makes a big difference. I grow a silver carpet of *Stachys lanata* (Lamb's Ears) underneath, which sets the flowers off wonderfully. The scent is really magnificent, too, which makes 'Empereur du Maroc' one of the most sublime roses overall. I'm always excited when I pick the first bloom of the season; I love burying my nose in the centre and inhaling its delicious perfume. The flowers hang slightly, which adds to their charm. I rate this as one of the most exquisite roses in my garden.

DIRECTORY p141

Guinée

The colour of this climbing rose is so astonishing that it always catches visitors' attention. It has an amazing richness and quality that is a combination of dark scarlet and blood-red. The perfume from the flowers is gloriously sweet and pronounced and on a warm summer's day, when you're close up, it's quite intoxicating – exactly what you would imagine a red rose to smell like. I have seen a fantastic example of 'Guinée' growing in Carmel Duignan's garden in Shankill, near Dublin, where a deep purple clematis has been allowed to mingle through the upper part of the plant. The contrast between the rich purple and the darkest red is breathtaking. If possible, position it against a pale background otherwise the dark flowers will recede and disappear. DIRECTORY p159

Intrigue

I fell in love with this rose when I first came across it at the rose garden in St. Anne's Park in Raheny, north of Dublin. Here, a large bed was planted with about fifty specimens. The combination of small flowers, their great abundance, and the truly magnificent colour created a wonderful carpet-like effect. What also makes this rose so special are the strong stems, each of which carries so many flowers. These stems mean that it makes a superb cut flower. It's also blessed with an exceptionally vibrant red colouring and would make the perfect rose if you're planting a fiery colour scheme. What I particularly like is how the colour changes in different light; in dull light the flowers take on an almost sinister depth, whereas in full sunlight, the scarlet in the flower shines through. The same variation in colour tones can be seen at the different stages of the flower's development, being darkest as the buds just open, and paling just before the petals drop. The overall effect created by this rose is one of sheer luxury. That, together with its compact size and long flowering period, make it worthy of a centre-stage position. DIRECTORY p133

L.D. Braithwaite

I've always been thrilled by this amazing, full-flowered crimson rose bred by David Austin. It's a modern rose with a strong presence, but it oozes old-world character. The first time I saw it was in a photograph and I was blown away. It was pictured in a bowl with wild, ripe blackberries. I immediately coveted it and decided there and then that I was going to grow it. It looks fantastic when planted in groups of three or five, where you can really appreciate the full show that it is capable of giving. It makes a medium-sized bush and also looks great planted in a dramatic or hot-colour planting scheme in a mixed border. It's interesting that the scent is rather faint as the buds open, but it matures and develops along with the flower, giving a rich, old-fashioned rose perfume. It's one of those 'touchy-feely' roses that demands attention – the kind you simply want to hold in your hand. Perhaps it's the size of the flower that attracts me, for when it comes into flower each year for the first time, I just love to cup my hands around its blooms. DIRECTORY p141

William Shakespeare 2000

The first time David Austin released this rose, he was disappointed with its disease-resistance, so he withdrew it after a few years. He then relaunched this improved version with the new name of William Shakespeare 2000. This has the disease-resistance he was looking for and is now considered to be one of his masterpieces. In fact, in his own opinion – and mine – it is his most beautiful deep crimson English rose. It's the shape, colouring and scent of this amazing flower that make it universally appealing. Once you've seen it, you'll always recall it. The flower colour is a deep, rich crimson with violet, purple and lilac shading as the flowers mature, an effect that gradually changes the mood of the flower. Large, flat and open, with the petals turning back, the flowers form a perfect rosette. Once you smell it, you'll never forget it. It has a sweet, old-rose fragrance. What a sensation! If you only have space for one red rose, I recommend you put this one high on your list. Grow it once and you'll never want to be without it. It's a real treasure.

DIRECTORY p142

roses for shaded positions

We don't usually think of roses growing in shady spots. These areas of our gardens can be difficult to select flowers for, but here are some excellent roses you might like to try. They all tolerate shade.

Madame Alfred Carrière

I'm often asked to recommend a climbing or rambling rose suitable for a north-facing wall and this is always the first to come to mind. It really is a splendid plant. In the shade of a north wall, its bright, double white flowers, flushed lightly with pink, shine against the dark green foliage. It establishes quickly and is fast-growing. It's a rose I remember well from my grandmother's garden, where it rambled over part of an old hedge. I recall its particularly strong, wonderful fruity fragrance with hints of musk, which is the reason I still grow it today. In full flower it always transports me back to happy childhood days. I really cannot recommend this rose highly enough. It blooms continuously throughout the summer, producing its flowers freely. It has disease-resistant foliage and is a hardy rose that you can count on as being reliable. Introduced in 1879, it is still supremely popular today. In short, it's my top choice for a shaded or north-facing wall. DIRECTORY p154

Mermaid

This is a classic climbing rose with exquisitely beautiful, soft primrose-yellow single flowers with golden central stamens, which unfurl from perfectly pointed buds. The flowers have a light fragrance and are produced continuously through the summer. They are set against dark green, glossy foliage. Its beauty most definitely lies in its colour and simplicity of flower. I have seen it growing very well in shaded positions and it is an equally good rose for security. I first saw it grown to perfection in the late John Conan's garden, near Bray, south of Dublin. When I came across it, I remember being amazed at its vicious thorns, which are large and hooked. I remember John telling me that when he did any tidying or cutting back, it was like grappling with a vicious monster. Although 'Mermaid' is slow to get going initially, it will catch up in time and is well worth the wait. In full flower, this rose is a magnificent sight – really eye-catching and truly memorable. DIRECTORY p156

Golden Showers

This is one of the most widely available yellow modern climbing roses. Its flowers are large and double and its bright colour makes it an excellent choice for a shady spot where, in full flower, it adds a touch of sunlight. I once saw a specimen in John Bourke's Dublin garden at Fairfield Lodge, where it had been planted in a north-facing corner and was combined, very simply, with a large, topiarised golden privet. The combination was uplifting, transforming the shady corner into a bright and radiant spot. I've also seen it succesfully combined with a blue-flowered clematis where the colour contrast worked extremely well. It's an early flowerer, especially in a sunny, sheltered spot and the first flush of flowers is usually followed by several smaller flushes throughout the summer, until the first frosts. If this rose has a fault, I would say it's the fact that the blooms can become loose too early, and then the flowers lose their attractive, individual shape, but when viewed from a distance, this doesn't really matter. DIRECTORY p155

Climbing Étoile de Hollande

This certainly ranks among the very best of the double red climbing roses. Its flowers are large and develop from beautifully shaped buds and the foliage is dark green and glossy. The flower colour is a velvety red, rich and deep, with a fragrance to match. The first flush of flowers can be spectacular. After this, it produces a reasonable crop but, as the season progresses into autumn, I have found it to be a little unpredictable. 'Climbing Étoile de Hollande' has been grown in gardens since the 1930s and it is still popular today. I remember seeing it growing in a vineyard in France, where it had been positioned at the end of a row of fruiting grape vines. When I enquired about this, I was told that it was the practice in this vineyard to plant climbing roses in this way as an early-warning signal. If the rose becomes diseased, it indicates that the vines need attention. DIRECTORY p158

Climbing Madame Caroline Testout

This rose was named after a famous French couturier who came from Grenoble. She had a fashion house in Paris and another in London and was an astute businesswoman who understood how to market her gowns. With marketing in mind, she approached a rose breeder in Lyons, Joseph Pernet-Ducher, from whom she purchased the rose we know and love today. Pernet-Ducher agreed to name it after her and she launched it with her fashion collection in the late spring of 1890. It was a great hit at the time and people still grow this magnificent, strong-growing rose today. The climbing version was introduced in 1901. It does well in many Irish gardens but probably the most magnificent plant I know of is at Knockcree, the garden of John and Shirley Beatty in south Co. Dublin. There, it is grown to perfection against the gable end of the house which, in early summer, is smothered in large, rich rose-pink, blousy flowers. They are globular in shape and have a wonderful soft scent. In September, the rose gives a second crop. DIRECTORY p163

Handel

This marvellous climber was bred by McGredy of Northern Ireland and was greatly celebrated on its release. Its large double flowers – with their unique colouring of cream, edged with rose-pink to crimson – make it very special. The petals are also ruffled, which adds to the flowers' fullness. Handel has been popular since the mid-1960s and it is especially happy to grow in shaded spots where its light, pretty flowers help it to stand out. I've found it ideally suited to Irish weather conditions but

have also found that it can be a little slow to get established. So, in one garden, where it was needed on a north-facing wall that was seen from the house, I planted three together for greater impact and to give it a better-looking start. The result has been absolutely fantastic. The rose grows happily and its summer display is very much appreciated. Handel also makes an excellent cut flower, as the flowers are produced on long stems and last well in water, while its unusual colouring gives the flower arranger plenty of opportunities to experiment.

DIRECTORY p165

roses for hedges

Roses make excellent hedging plants – maybe not the conventional choice, but they form attractive divisions between areas of the garden. Thorny varieties are particularly good for use as security hedging.

Nevada

I remember attending a lecture given by the great rosarian Graham Stuart Thomas, during which he showed a slide of a mature specimen of 'Nevada' growing in his own garden. It was an absolute knockout. The very next day, I bought it and planted it, and have never regretted it, as it has completely lived up to the image I had seen. I have now really enjoyed growing this rose for many years and have tried it with various companions. As a hedge it makes a great backdrop for plants, such as sky-blue delphiniums, and I have also seen 'Nevada' grown as an informal hedge, dividing different sections of a vegetable garden. This rose's large flowers are single to semi-double, opening ivory white and turning to pure white as they age. The central yellow stamens are exposed and it has a pleasing, attractive, light fragrance. I've grown this rose against a north wall for over twenty years and it rewards me with an annual summer display of white blossoms that cover the plant from top to bottom.

DIRECTORY p137

Alister Stella Gray

This is an exceptionally good Noisette rose, named after the son of a wealthy Scottish rose grower. It really responds well to being grown in a warm, sheltered, dry spot. In a wet climate, its delicate petals will suffer. The flowers start off a rich buff shade and, as they unfurl, they fade to white. As the weather gets cool in autumn, the flower colour deepens. The beauty of this rose lies in its flower formation – a central button eye surrounded by scrolled petals, forming a quartered shape. Some find the flower shape untidy but I think it has a great informal beauty. The flowers are carried in clusters of between six and eight on the first flowering and can have as many as thirty on the stronger flower-producing growth in early autumn. The scent is strong and musky and will carry on a light breeze. The foliage is light green and fairly glossy. 'Alister Stella Gray' makes an excellent climber which, when trained, can reach five metres. It can also be grown as a shrub and, with some support, you might like to try it as an informal hedge, or even for training up a wall. It would look splendid if you want to create an old-world cottage-garden look. I have seen it used to great effect to divide a vegetable garden. There is also the advantage of it having few thorns, which makes it easier to deal with as a hedging plant. DIRECTORY p155

Frühlingsgold

One of the earliest-flowering roses I grow is 'Frühlingsgold' which, in a sheltered spot, flowers in early May. The flowers are bright and cheery and a real joy. When I see them, I know that they herald the main flush of my rose garden. 'Frühlingsgold' made its debut in 1937 and is recognised as one of the finest roses to have been introduced by the great rose breeders, Kordes. When you see a large bush or even a hedge of this rose in full flower, you'll be entranced. The branches are festooned and weighed down with rich, cream to yellow flowers with an attractive and somewhat saucer-like shape. They range from near single to semi-double. The fragrance is good and when you are close up, it carries on the air. One sad note is that it only flowers for a few weeks; in my garden, I get no more than two weeks from it, but what a glory those two weeks are. If you are planting it as a hedge, give each plant ample space to develop and avoid overcrowding. That way you will be able to appreciate the beauty of its natural form. DIRECTORY p138

Charles de Mills

Introduced in 1790, this is one of my favourite Gallica roses. I fall in love with it again and again each summer. Its colour and the shape of its flowers are what make it a favourite. One of the finest specimens that I know and I admire is in Helen Dillon's Dublin garden. Previously called 'Bizarre Triomphant', this rose is one of the most popular of the old-fashioned roses and when you see a bush in full flower you'll know why. The flowers are large and magnificent. Each bloom, when fully open, is flat and divided into quarters as if someone had trimmed them with a sharp knife. As the flowers mature, they resemble the inside of an overblown Portobello mushroom. The colour is a delicate concoction of crimson with purple tones, plum with hints of violet, and cerise with undertones of red. The flowers hold well on the bush and also last well as cut flowers. The scent is light and sweet, floral and resinous. The growth can be a little lax so the plant will benefit from the occasional bamboo cane for staking. However, once established, 'Charles de Mills' will sucker, making a full thicket that is perfect for hedging, as well as a specimen in a mixed border.

DIRECTORY p143

Bonica

I first saw this rose when I was on a visit to some private Dutch gardens. A group of three had been planted together, forming a dense, even, bushy plant that was smothered from top to bottom in gorgeous pink flowers. Since then, I have added several groups of it to my own garden and have been really pleased with its performance. It makes a tidy, bushy plant that is perfect for stunning low-growing hedges, as you are guaranteed a plentiful show of blooms and colour. It can also be used to great

effect in mixed border plantings. The flowers are a sugar pink, though the buds are a deeper shade. In warmer climates, it keeps its colour best if planted with a little shade. This rose has a very long flowering period and, after its long first flush, you can expect a continuation of fewer flowers well into autumn. Red-orange hips are produced in winter, adding to the display. You can also expect a soft and pleasant fragrance. In my opinion, this rose offers excellent value and is ideally suited for planting in small gardens. It's one I'm happy to recommend highly. DIRECTORY p148

Felicia

'Felicia' is one of my favourite Hybrid Musk roses and has been growing in gardens since 1928. I remember seeing bushes of it festooned with flowers at the gardens of Ballymaloe Cookery School many years ago. These gardens were created by the famous Irish cook Darina Allen, who uses roses extensively throughout the gardens. The 'Felicia' plants were grown in large containers and gave a spectacular welcome as you drove in. The flowers are produced in clusters along the stem, starting as buds that are crimson in colour and opening to loose double flowers which are a rich rose-pink with apricot tones. The backs of the petals are flushed with apricot and salmon. The overall combination of colours is very pleasing and the dark-green foliage acts as an excellent foil to the abundance of pink flowers. The scent is sweet, strong and musky, and carries on the air. I have been told that 'Felicia' makes an excellent hedge and I plan on trying it for myself. The blooms are also excellent as a cut flower, as they last well in water and you can really appreciate the scent close up. The flowers start in June and will continue abundantly all the way through summer. In autumn, you can expect a great flush of flowers and I have even seen 'Felicia' looking well in the middle of November. DIRECTORY p146

roses for security
(impenetrable barriers)

These roses have especially nasty sharp thorns, making them an ideal choice for use as security plants. Few burglars will attempt to tackle any of these!

R. sericea subsp. *omeiensis* f. *pteracantha*

Here is a rose that nobody in their right mind will argue with. It displays its rather vicious-looking thorns quite openly and it is for the beauty and effect its thorns create that it is grown, rather than for its flowers. I can think of nothing prettier than the sight of sunlight catching the new thorns, which glow and shine a translucent bright red. These are a marvellous contrast to its soft, ferny foliage. Specimens should be pruned in winter to encourage new growth in spring, for it is this that will carry the fresh, bright red thorns. By the end of the season they will have turned a silver-grey colour. This rose does produce flowers, though these are small and only have four petals, which is something unique to it. Their colour is cream, fading to white, and they are usually carried in small clusters. In a warm sheltered spot, it will flower early though, as I say, the flowers are not the main reason for growing this rose. If the plant is well cared for and good growing conditions are provided, it will grow strongly. It's extremely tolerant of poor soil conditions and, when grown as a hedge, it provides an impenetrable barrier that will deter even the most persistent of burglars. This really is a rose with a difference. DIRECTORY p137

Saint Swithun

Named to commemorate the nine-hundredth anniversary of Winchester Cathedral and introduced by David Austin in 1993, Saint Swithun was the result of a cross between a Noisette Rose and one of David Austin's old rose hybrids. It is one of the thornier English roses whose growth is tall, vigorous and upright, yet with careful pruning it's easy to keep it as a tidy bush. In bush form, you might like to try it as a hedge or you may wish to combine it with the climbing form. Whichever you choose, it certainly provides a thorny barrier that's difficult for anyone to pass through. Saint Swithun is a magnificent rose that produces very large blooms in a lovely soft pink colour. Each bloom is open and cupped and absolutely full of petals. The colour fades gently to white at the edges of the flower. I would say that this rose provides the most attractive garden security you can imagine. DIRECTORY p147

Souvenir de Georges Pernet

A burglar would be very reluctant to climb over a thorny plant, so any climbing rose with thorns provides excellent security. Here I indulge myself by recommending one that isn't widely available, but which I love dearly. 'Souvenir de Georges Pernet' is a great favourite of mine and it's sad to think that it has almost disappeared from cultivation. Less than a handful of rose growers offer it in their catalogues today, one of which is Roseraie de Berty in France (see Resources, page 184). In June it produces a magnificent display of huge, blousy, almost vulgar pink flowers that are reminiscent of peonies. The scent is soft and light, rather than particularly strong, but the plant makes up for this with its eye-catching colour and size of flower. The foliage is mid-green and glossy, while the stems are, of course, thorny. You'll need a strong support to hold the weight of this rose, particularly when it's in full flower. I'd love to see it more widely grown. It has great strength and character and deserves to be in many more gardens. DIRECTORY p164

best thornless roses

If you'd like to choose a rose for growing over an arch or close
to a doorway, it's useful to select one that doesn't have thorns that
could snag or tear clothing. These beautiful roses are ideal as
they produce few, if any, thorns.

Cardinal de Richelieu

This is a wonderful old Gallica rose from the
1840s. Almost thornless, its name conjures up
images of the fabulously coloured robes worn
by cardinals. The flower is an amazing
ecclesiastical purple – just imagine the deepest,
darkest purple and you've got the idea – and
the texture and quality of its petals give the
impression that they've been cut from the
finest silk taffeta. The flowers take on an
antique quality as they mature, when mauve,
purple and grey tones shade the petals. They
are particularly attractive at this stage. The
foliage is dark green and acts as a good foil
for the beautiful colour of the flowers. The
whole combination is really exquisite.
I remember seeing 'Cardinal de Richelieu'
grown to perfection in Rosemary Brown's
garden at Graigueconna, Co. Wicklow. It was
just one of a large collection of old roses that
she had gathered together over many years.
The scent is light and delicious with an
undertone of honey. One disadvantage I have
found is that 'Cardinal de Richelieu' is rather
light and thin in its growth and it requires
some care. For the best display of flowers,
it needs good cultivation and appreciates
regular feeding. If you are prepared to feed it
generously it will, in return, reward you with
plenty of flowers. DIRECTORY p142

Veilchenblau

This is a rose I had seen growing in many gardens – Mottisfont and Sissinghurst come to mind. But I became more intimately acquainted with it in Carmel Duignan's garden south of Dublin, where she grows it to perfection on a south-facing wall at the back of her house. It's really hard to miss it, with its flowers produced in plentiful bunches. In full flower, it is the most exquisite colour imaginable. The buds open from rich magenta and quickly change to a violet-blue tone, which is difficult to describe. The flowers eventually fade to a lilac-grey colour before the petals drop. The fragrance is also very special – it's like a sweet scent of oranges. I have recently planted this rose on a pergola in the centre of my garden. It's an area where quite a lot of people pass by, so I was anxious to include a rose that produced no thorns. 'Veilchenblau' was my immediate choice. The combination of no thorns, exquisite colouring and scent of oranges meant it was perfect for me. It's a sophisticated rose and one that really should be treasured. DIRECTORY p160

Reine des Violettes

I recall pressing the great rosarian Graham Stuart Thomas to pick a favourite from his encyclopaedic knowledge of rose varieties. He laboured for a few minutes and told me if he were to choose one rose above and beyond all others it would be 'Reine des Violettes'. This is a rose I then planted and immediately understood why he loved it so much – its remarkable colouring, the shape of its flower and its old-fashioned appeal. The large double flowers open a gorgeous deep pink, and then turn a soft, gentle violet, shading to lilac and gradually paling with age to a divine lilac-grey. These full, open blooms are one of the true joys of the summer garden and the colouring is so unusual – it's the sort of shade you'd expect to find on a piece of antique Venetian velvet. What is more, the scent of this rose is strong and delicious. It's what I would call a really sophisticated rose. To grow it to its peak of perfection, plant it in a sheltered spot with plenty of sunshine and richly cultivated soil. It responds well to kindness and you'll find that feeding and good cultivation make all the difference. Your extra effort will be rewarded by its flowers, which are a treasure in any garden. I've included 'Reine des Violettes' in several gardens that I've designed, placing it in mixed borders containing many old-fashioned herbaceous perennials. It adds its own personal, old-world character. In one garden I planted it close to a large clump of *Alchemilla mollis*. The frothy, lime-green flowers combine wonderfully with this rose – you might like to try this combination yourself. DIRECTORY p143

James Galway

Somehow or other, classical music and old-fashioned roses seem to belong together, so when I heard that there was a rose named in honour of James Galway, the world's greatest flautist, I knew I just had to have it. I had met James many years before. It was just as he was heading off on a trip to Japan and we had a long chat about his interest in gardening, especially bonsai, so I was keen to include the rose named after him in my own collection. I planted it, looked forward to it flowering and can say that I wasn't disappointed. It produces stunning, shapely blooms with an almost perfectly formed old-fashioned rose shape. The flowers are packed full of petals placed in perfect symmetry and the result is a sumptuous-looking rose. The colouring in the centre of each bloom is a medium pink, the outer petals fading to a soft, creamy pink. The combination is gorgeous. Its growth is upright and, after growing it for a number of years now, I'm delighted to say that in my own garden there has been no sign of disease. I grow it against a low trellis where it makes an attractive short climber. I make a point of feeding it well every year and it responds with a magnificent display of flowers. It's also one of my favourite roses for cutting. It may not have the best scent – the fragrance is light – but it certainly is one of the most attractive-looking roses. It is yet another one of David Austin's masterpieces, and to top all this off, it produces no thorns. DIRECTORY p147

Zéphirine Drouhin

This is one of the most widely grown Bourbon roses. The flowers have beautiful buds and open gracefully, but sadly they become rather loose, as if overblown. However, I don't let this worry me, as the bright, rich pink colour is so good and it's very much appreciated when seen from a distance. But what is most important is to get close to this rose because its scent is truly delicious. It can only be described as a penetrating perfume with strong notes of crushed raspberries and fruit. It's an excellent climbing rose that is happy to grow in the shade of a north wall and it produces no thorns. You can even try it as a hedge or a freestanding shrub. It responds well when grown in good soil conditions and if you have a sunny, sheltered spot with good soil, and are prepared to look after it by feeding and watering it well, I can promise you that you will never regret planting it. I often cut the flowers and bring them inside to enjoy their exquisite, rich perfume. As it was one of the first roses I every planted, it holds a special place in my heart. For me, this rose in full flower is the epitome of summer. DIRECTORY p165

roses for growing in trees

Here is a selection of roses that are large enough and strong enough to be grown through trees. The effect they create when mature, can be stunning. If it's a romantic look you want, grow one of these through an old apple tree.

Albéric Barbier

I always think that a rose growing up through and flowering in an old tree can help to extend colour and interest in the garden, as well as contributing a romantic atmosphere. There are few roses that are better at doing this than 'Albéric Barbier' and I've recently planted one to grow up through an old apple tree myself. It has a strong, upright growth and is capable, with a little help, of working its way through even a large tree. With careful attention and a little patience, it will make a magnificent display, giving the impression that the tree is in full flower. 'Albéric Barbier' is a Wichuriana rose and probably one of the best you can grow. It's also one of the most popular of rambling roses. My grandmother grew and loved it and I often see it growing over low walls in the coastal gardens of south Co. Dublin. It's also very suitable for growing over a pergola. Tolerant of shade, some of the best plants I've seen have been on a north-facing wall. The buds are a rich butter-yellow, opening to fully double, creamy white flowers, dark in the centre and paling towards the edge of the petals. The flowers are produced in small clusters. This rose has a reputation for growing well in poor soils, so it won't mind competing with the roots of the tree. However, until it's established, I do suggest some feeding to encourage a good, strong, healthy root system. DIRECTORY p154

Félicité Perpétue

If you're looking for a strong rambling rose, you'll find it hard to beat this one. Its combination of great vigour and beauty make it a climbing rose classic. The flowers open from tight crimson buds. This colour rapidly changes, eventually turning shell-pink and, as they develop, the flowers slowly change and lighten in colour, turning from a rose-cream to a soft pink-white. The flower clusters are full and there can be as many as forty or fifty at any one time, creating a real burst of opulence. In addition, the fragrance is very pleasing – sweet and musky. This excellent and reliable rambler is happy to be grown even in shady spots or in poor soil and is excellent if you let it ramble through a pergola or up into a tree, though it needs a strong support. Here it is shown growing through a *Philadelphus*, a sweetly-scented shrub. 'Félicité Perpétue' only flowers once in the season, but it would be a pity not to grow it just because of that, for in full flower its showy display is second to none. This old rose is worthy of any garden. It never disappoints and always looks cheerful and summery.

DIRECTORY p162

R. banksiae Lutea

This stunning rambler was introduced from Nanking in China in 1824 and is believed to be an old Chinese garden hybrid. In early summer, it produces a profusion of clusters of very double, warm-yellow flowers with a small green eye at the centre of each flower. The single-flowered form has a scent of violets but there's only a hint of scent from this double form. It's excellent for growing up into trees where, once established, it can reach about ten metres. It needs sunshine and, if possible, should be planted a little distance from the tree so that it's not competing for moisture or food. In Irish gardens it needs a sheltered sunny spot, as the young growth can be hit by late frosts. There is a magnificent example at Fernhill, Sandyford, Co. Dublin where it grows on a sheltered wall of the house. It's a glorious sight in full flower. The colouring of the flowers is so soft and the flowers so small and double that it gives a hazy effect when seen from a distance. Stunningly beautiful, this rose is a real garden treasure and is deserving of the best care and attention.

DIRECTORY p155

Climbing Cécile Brünner

This was first introduced to me by the late John Conan, a great gardener who adored roses. It was one of his favourites. The climbing form is an excellent choice for growing into trees, as it has a strong and vigorous growth. Expect its first flush of flowers to appear in June. It usually then produces flowers sporadically for the rest of the season. The flowers grow in large clusters typical of a Polyantha, with anything from twelve to twenty flowers per cluster. On close inspection, each flower resembles a perfectly formed miniature Hybrid Tea. I love the way the flowers unfold from the pointed buds. The colour is a warm coral-pink which gradually shades to a softer, paler pink and then to white at the edges. The colour fades more quickly in full sunlight than in shade. If you want to grow this rose and don't have the space for a climber, you might consider its bush form, which grows to around one metre in height. Once it is established and happy in its position, it will produce a main flush of its sweetly scented blooms followed by more blooms intermittently throughout the season. Finally, if you're looking for a buttonhole rose, this one is perfect. It's the right size and shape and the flowers are charming. DIRECTORY p160

Doctor W. Van Fleet

This rose certainly ranks highly in my list of top choices for growing through a tree. It's not seen so much in catalogues now, as it has been superseded by its sport 'New Dawn', but I do believe it's still worth hunting for, especially if you need a rose to grow through a tree. It is

absolutely glorious when you see it in full flower. Popular for years in Ireland, it is a feature of gardens both north and south. It is extra-vigorous in its growth, with sharp thorns that help it scramble through the tree. The flesh-pink, double, very sweetly scented flowers are small and are produced in great quantities. Your breath will be taken away when you see it blooming in the branches of a tree. The rich, dark, glossy green foliage is also very good. 'Doctor W. Van Fleet' really is too vigorous for the smaller garden; if you plant one there, your home could end up surrounded by thorny stems, like Sleeping Beauty's castle, but where space allows, and if you have an appropriate tree, this is the rose to grow. Make sure you feed it well so that it doesn't suffer from the competition. DIRECTORY p162

roses for trailing over walls

These roses can make a striking impact when allowed to trail over walls. A tumbling display of colour will add a dramatic and vivid touch to your garden.

Albertine

This is one of the many roses I have had a love affair with. I had a friend who loved it so much that he insisted on planting it in his tiny town-house garden, which was about the size of a postage stamp. The rose was planted in pride of place and there he left it to grow, and grow, and grow. After a couple of years, he couldn't get into the garden, and all because he adored it so much that he refused to prune or train it. So I implore you not to plant 'Albertine' in a tiny space. Give it a little bit of room, keep it tidy, and it will reward you with a stunning display in early June. The buds are an amazing shade of rich salmon-pink and, as they unfold, you see the sort of colours you find on the inside of a conch shell – orange, apricot and coral – all blended together. Eventually, they open to pure pink, with a divine scent. In full flower, this is one of the most sublime roses imaginable. The best display I have ever seen was growing over a low wall on top of a bank. The rose was allowed to trail over both wall and bank and created a curtain of colour when in full bloom. It was truly magnificent.

DIRECTORY p161

Raubritter

This rose has great character and a look all of its own. In full flower, it's so distinctive that it is recognisable even from a distance, thanks to the shape of the flowers. The buds are small and pointed, then they unfurl into small, globular-shaped blooms which are open at the top. The colour is a deep pink, much of which is hidden inside the globe, but the reverse of the petal, which is exposed because of the globular shape, is a pale, soft, silver-pink. It's a very profuse flowerer with clusters bearing up to forty flowers. It is happiest in dry weather, as otherwise the leaves can be susceptible to blackspot and mildew. 'Raubritter' can be grown as a climber, and I have also seen it grown as ground cover with its stems pinned to the ground, but I suggest that you allow it to trail over a low wall. This lifts the plant off the ground and showcases its unusual flowers. Sadly, these only appear once in the season, but what a display they offer! The effect is truly luxuriant and, grown this way, I think you get the full benefit as the flowers are closer to you. It's a very striking rose and when you see one grown at its best, you're sure to remember it. DIRECTORY p149

Paul Transon

This is a charming rambling rose with such character that it's instantly recognisable. It produces a good display of flowers that are exquisite in shape, colour and fragrance. They appear in small clusters and are fully double, with each packed full of small petals that are quilled and sometimes quartered. They are a gorgeous colour – salmon-pink with copper and orange tones, which makes a beautiful combination. The scent is reminiscent of a freshly peeled apple – fruity and uplifting. It's a rose that is happy to grow in sun or shade and it flowers continuously well into autumn. Its growth is strong and vigorous, with the new growth tinged copper-red. The leaves eventually become a dark, glossy green. It's sometimes prone to mildew but this is usually late in the season and never causes any great harm. I've seen it grown beautifully at Giverny, near Paris, the garden planted by the great French artist, Claude Monet, and have also seen it grown along a low wall surrounding a paddock at a farmhouse. It stretched for about five metres along the top of the wall and was an amazing sight. In that position it was really possible to appreciate its wonderful strong scent of apples. DIRECTORY p158

Flower Carpet Pink

While travelling through France, I've often seen this planted in great quantities in the middle of roundabouts. So dazzling is it in full flower that I'm amazed that motorists aren't distracted and don't collide with each other. I'm fond of Flower Carpet but not on roundabouts. It's very popular in Ireland and it deserves its popularity, as it's easy to grow, has a natural trailing habit, is happy to flower in great profusion and is very rewarding. I have grown the pink form on a raised bed, allowing it to fall over the wall, which is roughly one metre high. There are very few plants in the surrounding area, which is probably a good idea as Pink Flower Carpet is a diva who likes to be centre stage. The colour of this rose is best appreciated, I think, without competition from other colours or, should I say, without *it* competing with other colours! However, if you decide to grow it with other flowers in close proximity, I find it best to use plants with colours that are rich enough to hold their own. Here the rose is grown with *Fuchsia* 'Genii' for dramatic impact. Flower Carpet roses are available in different colours. I have tried most of them but the pink form has proved to be the most prolific flowerer for me. DIRECTORY p150

Phyllis Bide

This is a very lovable rose which looks glorious, especially from a distance, when its apricot, peach, gold and pink colouring merges into a soft mélange. On close inspection, the strange shape of the flowers can look untidy, a bit like blown miniature Hybrid Tea roses, but I think they're charming. For years, this rose was one of the highlights at the entrance to Helen Dillon's garden in Ranelagh, Dublin, where it festooned an old iron gate, garlanding it with its pretty flowers in early summer. It was a real sight to behold and what a welcome as you arrived. The flower clusters are very profuse, with up to perhaps thirty flowers in each, and it blooms continuously through the season, seeming to be always in flower. The foliage is small and generally healthy. 'Phyllis Bide' makes a charming, low-growing rambler and would look super trained over a low wall, where you would get a cascading effect. It's a pity this rose isn't more widely seen. It has stood the test of time and is still worthy of a place in even the smallest garden.

DIRECTORY p165

roses for pergolas and arches

One of the most striking ways to display roses in your garden is on pergolas or arches. You can really appreciate the full effect of a climbing or rambling rose when it is grown and supported in this way.

A Shropshire Lad

Here is a rose with a wonderful fragrance – delicious, sweet and fruity. The scent belongs to the Tea rose tradition. It's one of David Austin's most beautiful climbing roses – and a reliable one, too – which looks fantastic when grown over an arch. It's a strong grower and, with good feeding, will provide an excellent crop of cup-shaped flowers in a combination of delicate peach and pink. I love the way the flowers fade in colour towards the edges of the petals and the outer parts of the flower. As the crop of flowers can be quite heavy, it's important to ensure that the rose is properly secured to its support. I've seen A Shropshire Lad growing on walls, where it provides a spectacular show when well cared for, but it can also be grown as a large freestanding shrub that features attractive arching growth. Grown this way, you can appreciate how the flowers are displayed on the nodding stems. It likes adequate moisture in summer and responds well to being mulched. If you're planting it on an arch of any size, it's best to use several plants to ensure a full display from the base upwards. DIRECTORY p144

The Generous Gardener

Introducing an arch into your garden can add instant height, which is especially valuable if you're restricted on space. If you're thinking of doing this, you might like to consider growing this fabulous rose. It's one of the most beautiful and romantic of all the climbing roses. Soft, shell-pink, delicate petals, which fade to almost white, make up sumptuous cup-shaped flowers that open to expose the central stamens. David Austin describes the flowers as being like waterlilies. To add to their charm, the flowers nod gently from their stems, creating a billowing effect. There is a spicy quality to the fragrance of this rose; it's a combination of scents such as myrrh and musk with the added sweetness of old rose. Though the flowers have a delicate, ethereal quality, the plant is quite strong-growing and makes an excellent climber. Introduced in 2002, it is highly disease-resistant and is one of the best newer climbing roses to come on the market. In full flower, this looks rather special and one I believe we're going to see more of. I wouldn't be surprised if it ends up becoming a real classic. DIRECTORY p161

Baltimore Belle

To see this gorgeous rambling rose in full flower is a spectacular sight. Its small, very double flowers are produced abundantly and in large clusters. The fragrance is light and musky. The centre of each flower is button-shaped and you will sometimes find a small green eye. Before the buds open, they are often flushed crimson, and you may find that the unfolding flowers are pale pink in colour at first. As they open, they fade to a glorious pure white. The combination of buds, half-open buds and flowers in full bloom creates a striking effect somewhat reminiscent of a cherry-blossom tree. I have seen 'Baltimore Belle' grown in a garden outside Paris where it enjoys the heat and sunshine of the summer. Produced in the United States in 1843, this rose is greatly celebrated because it produces its flowers late in the season, often carrying them through into late August. It's also noted for being very hardy. It is happy to grow in light shade and is an excellent rose for training over an arch. What is more, the foliage is of good quality and has good resistance to disease. DIRECTORY p161

Blairii Number Two

I have used this large-flowered rose with stunning blooms to great effect over an archway, while a good friend of mine has planted it very successfully to frame a cottage door. The strong, sweetly scented, large flowers are a good pink colour, fading to a paler shade of pink towards the edges. Sometimes you'll find hints of lilac and grey. In full flower it is a magnificent sight and is one of the most beautiful roses I know. The flowers are also excellent for cutting, as they last well in water. It's a rose which is best pruned lightly and I have found that it can take a few years to settle in before it starts to give its good display. But position it carefully and give it rich soil, and you'll have an excellent rose for growing over arches and pergolas, as well as over doorways. Used in this way, you'll be able to inspect its blooms at close quarters. It has a reputation for being susceptible to mildew and blackspot but, with careful cultivation and good feeding, it will provide a great display. 'Blairii Number One', raised by the same breeder, is reputed to be a better rose for repeat-flowering, but I'm afraid it is rare and hard to find. You definitely won't be disappointed by 'Blairii Number Two'. DIRECTORY p161

Cornelia

This is a rose I remember from my mother's garden, where it was trained on a freestanding trellis and allowed to intermingle with late-flowering clematis. It always added a splash of colour to the summer garden. It produces small, tidy double flowers which are carried in large clusters of up to thirty. These extremely freely produced flowers open from coral-coloured buds and are a soft pink when they're in full flower, gradually fading to creamy pink. They're attractive all the way through, from the bud until just as the petals fall. With a little support, 'Cornelia' can be grown as a freestanding bush. I've even seen it growing in large tubs, where it was extremely eye-catching. But I especially like it trained as a Climber, when it can reach up to four metres in height. It looks particularly splendid grown over an archway, where the abundance of its flowers can really be appreciated. I just love the way it produces large sprays of blooms that hang on the plant. It's happiest in a warm, sunny, sheltered spot. The scent of the flowers is especially pervasive; it's best described as soft, rich and musky. In autumn, this rose produces a great flush and it's these flowers that I love to cut and bring into the house so I can really enjoy their scent close up. DIRECTORY p139

Debutante

It was after reading the description of this rose by Graham Stuart Thomas that I first decided I would try 'Debutante', and it's a decision I've never regretted. The flower colour is a lovely clear rose-pink that fades gradually to a soft creamy pink. When it's in full flower, the plant is covered in a profusion of flower clusters. Each bloom is small and fully double and, when completely open, it forms an attractive rosette. The plant is strong-growing but only flowers once. The fragrance of the flowers is particularly good – light, soft and musky, like the scent of a delicate primrose. 'Debutante' is regarded as one of the best pink rambling roses of its type – great for growing on arches and an excellent choice for a large wall in a sunny position. You may be forgiven for thinking at first sight that you're looking at 'Dorothy Perkins', but 'Debutante' is far more exceptional in every way. The foliage has good disease-resistance; it's rare for it to be attacked by mildew. This rose has been around since 1902, so it really has stood the test of time. I think it's sumptuously beautiful when grown over a pergola or large archway, where you can really appreciate its full display of flowers. DIRECTORY p162

roses for pots and containers

Growing roses in pots or containers allows you to have portable colour, as you can easily move the flowering rose to a spot where you can appreciate its full display. Growing in containers also allows you to enjoy roses where space is restricted.

Jacqueline du Pré

Jacqueline du Pré sports a large semi-double to single bloom of great charm and beauty. The colour is a creamy white and the reverse of the petals is a soft, glowing pale pink. This is a rose that looks magical when the blossoms are lit from behind by sunlight; every flower seems to glow like a bright orb. The long, salmon-pink filaments are dramatically positioned in the centre of the bloom, leading your eye in and enhancing the overall purity of the colour by contrast. The flowers appear in clusters of between three and twelve, the foliage is healthy and dark green, and the stems are prickly. Jacqueline du Pré needs deadheading after flowering and requires little pruning. In full flower this is a rose with a character all of its own. It's stunning grown in a pot or container, but make sure that the container is large enough, as this rose really resents the extremes of drought you can get if you use a small pot.

DIRECTORY p136

Little White Pet

This is a charming low-growing rose, and if you like the climber 'Félicité Perpétue', I know that you'll most definitely be bowled over by the beauty of this little gem. It's really the same but in miniature. Exquisite small pink buds open to double pompon-like white button-shaped flowers that are borne in upward-facing clusters. It's a fantastic rose for the front of borders and I've seen it used in several Irish gardens with great success, in one case for edging a path. I've also seen stunning short standards of this rose planted most effectively in John Bourke's white garden at Fairfield Lodge. This is a rose that will be continuously in flower well into autumn, especially if you deadhead the flowers and give it a liquid feed. 'Little White Pet' is also excellent grown in a large container. Always use the best-quality potting compost and make sure that the container has adequate drainage and is positioned in a bright, open spot. To sum up, this is a rose that has a very elegant, sophis-ticated appearance. Its proportions are beautiful and it always looks neat and tidy, which makes it a great rose for a small garden. DIRECTORY p136

Margaret Merril

If you're looking for a continuously flowering scented rose suitable for growing in a pot or container, you'll find it hard to beat Margaret Merril. It already ranks as one of the world's most popular Floribundas. The climate you grow it in can affect the colour of the flower; in cool climates, you can expect it to be the palest of pale pinks, whereas in warmer climates it is white. I always enjoy Margaret Merril early in the season, as it's one of the first Floribundas to flower. It produces its blooms in large clusters that continue all the way until the first frosts in late autumn. The flowers are large and semi-double and they form an attractive cup shape that exposes the stamens in the centre. The stamens carry buff-grey pollen, which is quite unusual for a rose. Margaret Merril can withstand rain very well and I always believe this to be a good quality, especially as I garden in the damp climate of Ireland. It produces very upright growth and is strong-growing and vigorous. The foliage is large and a dark, glossy green. If you garden in a warmer climate, it can be trained as a low-growing climber where it can reach between two and a half and three metres in height. I was originally sold this rose as a successor to Iceberg. In fact, it's completely different, but don't let that put you off. Margaret Merril has a lot of qualities and these, together with its strong, sweet scent – which Iceberg lacks – are good reason to try it.

DIRECTORY p130

Trumpeter

Trumpeter has become incredibly popular and it certainly deserves its place in gardens because of the value it offers. It's rare to find it without flower in summer and its neat, compact growth makes it ideal for planting in containers, especially large ones. It is also a super rose for edging a border or a driveway and I've seen it looking particularly good in this sort of situation at the rose garden in Tralee town centre, Co. Kerry. Planted in a large group, Trumpeter is particularly eye-catching – what you might call a real show-off rose. The flowers are semi-double to double, and are small and tidy. They're produced in plentiful quantity on trusses. The colour is a vibrant scarlet – a traffic-light red. The foliage is rich, green and healthy and the rose has good general disease-resistance. The height and spread of this rose make it ideally suited to smaller gardens where there may be pressure for space and it also adds a spectacular splash to a mixed border, where it can be planted towards the front. I've seen a very attractive planting combination, where it was planted next to *Lavandula* 'Hidcote'. The contrast of the purple lavender flowers with the vibrant red roses was extremely striking. DIRECTORY p132

Marian Finucane

There is a slow but constant stream of new Irish roses being bred. One of Ireland's leading rose breeders, David Kenny, launched this exquisite red Floribunda at the Garden Heaven Show in 2005. It had taken him five years to get this particular colour break – described as a bronze-red – in his breeding programme. It's this colour, together with the size and neat shape of this rose that make it special. The fully double flowers are exquisitely scented and produced in great abundance. The plants are neat, compact and tidy, which make them ideal for growing in containers, although they would also be very suited to a mixed border. 'Marian Finucane' has excellent disease-resistance too, and can be used as a cut flower, since the blossoms last well in water. Named after one of Ireland's best-loved radio and television personalities, for every rose sold, a donation will be given to Marian's favourite charity 'Friends in Ireland', which helps children orphaned by AIDS in South Africa. DIRECTORY p133

Sexy Rexy

This is a great award-winning Floribunda rose that has taken the world by storm. If you're looking for a quality rose, and one that's suitable for growing in containers, I can recommend it as I believe it offers great value. It makes a tidy plant and the colour and shape of the flower is good. It's healthy, with good foliage, and provides a great display. The flowers open to nearly flat with beautifully arranged petals resembling small, mid-pink camellias. The colour is a warm rose-pink and the petals are darker on the reverse. The scent is light and not particularly strong. I have found it is often late to come into flower, but it puts such energy into its first flush that it's worth waiting for. To encourage extra flowering, it's essential to deadhead. It looks great in mixed borders and I'd love it to be used more frequently in this way. You can see a magnificent display of Sexy Rexy at Sir Thomas and Lady Dixon Park in Belfast. If you plant it in a container for your patio or balcony, you'll be able to enjoy the wonderful symmetry of its flowers close up. For container growing, purchase the best-quality potting compost and, once it's established, give it a regular liquid feed. It will definitely appreciate this.

DIRECTORY p135

roses for poor soil conditions

In general, roses appreciate rich growing conditions. But there are roses which are tolerant of less fertile soil. This selection is suitable for the poorest soil quality.

Maigold

I have always loved this rose, especially as it's one of the earliest flowering of all the climbing roses. Its amazing display always started in a Dublin garden near to my childhood home around the middle of May. I've also noticed that the flowers can come even earlier if it's positioned in a warm, sheltered corner, preferably south-facing. The flower colour is golden-yellow with apricot and copper tones, and just before the flowers fall, they turn a pale, soft yellow. If the weather is cool, you'll find that the overall colour is stronger and darker. 'Maigold' is very tolerant of poor soils and is a very vigorous grower with thorny stems. It's a rose that really puts all of its energy into the first flush and its sumptuous display is a great way to kick-start the season. If, however, you want more flowers later in the season, you'll have to deadhead it. 'Maigold' looks great grown on pillars and arches; it needs a strong support. It has always been one of the most popular climbing roses, not, I think, for the shape of its flowers, but rather because of its early, cheerful display. Added to that, its fragrance is strong and sweet. I can think of nothing more pleasurable than seeing 'Maigold' in full flower at the start of the season.

DIRECTORY p157

Henri Martin

This is a really stunning Moss rose which has full, double, crimson flowers. It used to be called 'Old Red Moss' and then it received the name 'Henri Martin' in honour of a renowned French historian. Only flowering once a year, the flower is a light crimson-red and, as it ages, purple tones begin to appear, especially during hot spells. The centre of the flower sometimes reveals golden stamens. The flowers are grouped in clusters of between three and nine and, in autumn, you can enjoy the attractive, round, red rosehips. The buds are covered in light green moss. This particular rose is very tolerant of poor soil. I've even grown it in a coastal garden, where the soil was particularly sandy and poor. With careful annual mulching the rose responded well, making a dense, large plant. Its growth is long and arching and it looks fantastic when grown on a frame or tripod. This rose is also covered in thorns, making it a useful plant to prevent unwanted animals entering the garden. It's tough, fully hardy and, once established, tolerant of hot, dry conditions. The scent of the flowers is rich, with hints of citrus and orange and definite peppery tones. Try using it to add a real old-world touch, especially in a mixed border. It's one of the most beautiful Moss roses I have grown in my own garden. DIRECTORY p140

Complicata

There's a light airiness about 'Complicata' and a simplicity to its flowers that make it especially beautiful when in full bloom. The flowers are single, large and lightly cupped and they appear in clusters of up to five. They have a white centre with a boss of golden stamens. As the petals open, the outer parts are a rich rose-pink. The flowers have a light, sweet scent, their colour fading with age. 'Complicata' also produces wonderful red hips which make a fabulous addition to the autumn garden. It's not a particularly thorny rose and its habit is open and loose. It's possible to train it against a wall, where it can grow to a height of about three metres. Tolerant of poor soils, it enjoys a sunny aspect and needs good drainage. It also makes an excellent informal hedging plant. I've seen it used as a spot plant in a wildlife hedgerow that had been planted with single roses, honeysuckle and a mixture of native flowering plants. It really was striking and gave a huge visual uplift to the entire display.

DIRECTORY p148

American Pillar

To be honest, I can't say that this is a favourite rose of mine, but I've included it because of its popularity in old Irish gardens, especially in cottage gardens in the west and northwest, where the rich, deep pink colour of its flowers – each with a white central eye – really stands out against the whitewashed walls. The single flowers of this rambling rose, borne in clusters, are produced in great profusion in June and July and it's the combination of this profuse flowering and its tolerance of poor soil that give 'American Pillar' a place here. Sadly, it's not resistant to mildew and this can be a problem. Also, it's so vigorous in its growth that it needs serious training and pruning if it's to be kept in shape. If you're providing support for it, it needs to be seriously strong, as the stems are long and thick and very thorny. 'American Pillar' is easy to grow and propagate, and was usually passed from family to family as rooted cuttings. If you've got poor soil and want a rose that will quickly spread over walls and fences, then 'American Pillar' is the one for you. DIRECTORY p164

Mrs John Laing

I think this is a rose of great elegance. It flowers repeatedly through the whole summer and I've found it gives an especially good flush in autumn. The flowers are large and of a delicate, warm pink. When they're fully open they look slightly blousy, with a silver-pink tinge that gives a very pleasing effect. Their fragrance is opulent, rich and sweet, and the foliage is mid-green and generally healthy. It really is a very beautiful rose. The plant is upright in its growth and produces very few thorns, and the large flowers are heavy, sometimes weighing the branches over, so a little prudent staking with bamboo canes is a good idea. It's a very healthy plant, rarely suffering from disease and will tolerate poor soil, but I do recommend looking after it by feeding it well. It will respond by giving you an even healthier, more vibrant plant with a better quality of flower, and more of them. It looks fabulous planted in mixed borders. I believe it really must be considered one of the great old roses. DIRECTORY p149

Bourbon Queen

This is one of the most freely flowering of the old-fashioned roses and it's one you often come across in old Irish gardens. It can also be found listed under the name 'Reine de l'Île de Bourbon'. Very much appreciated for its rich, sweet fragrance, its flowers are a strong pink with a hint of purple, and in the centre of each you'll find a white patch. The reverse of the petals are a paler pink. This rose produces a really generous display of flowers which appear in small clusters. If you don't deadhead it, it will provide attractive, large orange rosehips that extend the period of interest into autumn and winter. It's a rose that's very tolerant of poor soils and neglect, which may account for its survival in many old estates and gardens around Ireland. Generally, it produces only one flush of flowers each year, but occasionally you may get a few blooms in late autumn. In warm climates this rose can be grown as a climber, where it can reach a height of around four metres. It's always been an old cottage-garden favourite, as it works superbly planted in among perennials. In association with sky-blue delphiniums, it's a truly magnificent sight. It really benefits from being mulched well, to keep in moisture in summer. DIRECTORY p150

roses for seaside locations

If you garden by the sea, you'll be well aware that salt-laden air can cause great difficulties when growing plants. This is a selection of roses which are tolerant of seaside garden conditions.

Blanche Double de Coubert

A favourite of the writer and gardener Vita Sackville-West, this is a rose which grows superbly in coastal gardens. Trouble-free and noted for its disease-resistance, it makes an excellent informal hedge and its purest white double flowers have a rich, sweet, strong fragrance, reminiscent of lily-of-the-valley. Apart from its gorgeous flowers that bloom continuously, starting with a first flush of in June, I love its wrinkled and pleated leaves. These turn a rich, bright, golden yellow in autumn. It also produces large orange hips in autumn and into early winter. This is a remarkable rose with many uses. I think, possibly, its only downside is the fact that the flowers are susceptible to rain damage. It is probably the most popular of the Rugosas and is widely available, and the fact that it doesn't need to be sprayed for disease is a big plus, especially if you practise organic cultivation methods. It makes an excellent specimen plant, can be grown as a hedge and looks especially good when planted with warm-coloured perennials. I'm particularly fond of that autumn foliage. DIRECTORY p136

Agnes

This rose was bred in 1900 but didn't appear in gardens until 1922. It is one of the great roses to come from Canada. It flowers early and is extremely hardy, and the flowers are a soft, pale yellow. As the buds open, they reveal a wonderful amber tone in the centre of each flower. The flowers are very beautiful but, sadly, they tend to collapse in wet weather. What makes up for this, I find, is the fact that 'Agnes' flowers over a long period. The flower stems are short and arching, with blooms usually appearing singly along them. The foliage is an attractive bright green, and the leaves are small and rough. 'Agnes' can suffer from blackspot or rust but if this appears, it's usually late in the season and doesn't really affect the performance of the plant the following year. The unusual scent is light and fruity – almost edible – but you need to get close to the blossoms to really appreciate it qualities. 'Agnes' is a Rugosa hybrid which, like its Rugosa parent, is happy in coastal areas. You can grow it as an informal hedge, but it looks particularly well as a specimen.

DIRECTORY p137

Mrs Anthony Waterer

This is one of the earliest Rugosa hybrids. It's an excellent choice as a hedging rose and will do very well in coastal areas. The flowers are bright crimson and, as they mature, they tone down, with the crimson taking on a lavender tinge. It produces great quantities of these semi-double flowers and they have a rich, pleasant perfume, as is the case with so many Rugosa roses. The foliage is rich green and corrugated, and the normally long, arching stems are particularly prickly. It's a handsome rose in flower and makes an attractive specimen plant. I really enjoy the first flush of flowers on this plant; it makes a truly splendid display. It repeat-flowers thereafter but never gives a great show in autumn. I recommend a light pruning at the end of winter but don't cut it hard back as it can take time to recover, sometimes at the expense of flowers. A happy plant can grow as much as two metres wide, so you need to give it a little bit of room if you're to appreciate its arching branches. They look truly magnificent when covered with flowers.

DIRECTORY p141

Roseraie de l'Haÿ

This is a fantastic, trouble-free rose, marvellous for coastal gardens and also superb as an informal hedge. I've seen it growing in gardens in the west of Ireland, exposed to sea salt and everything else the Atlantic Ocean can throw in its direction. I've also seen it growing well in a small coastal garden in Co. Wexford, where it was used as a hedge that was part of a windbreak. The purple-cerise scroll-shaped buds open to bright magenta-pink flowers, which are single to semi-double in form. The petals are ruffled and the scent is thick, rich and very sweet. The foliage is always healthy and disease-free. It is bright green and has a corrugated texture. The autumn colour of the foliage is also particularly good; it turns bright gold before it falls. 'Roseraie de l'Haÿ' does produce hips – not as many as other Rugosas, but they do add to the display in the late autumn and winter garden. The plant makes a good, bushy habit and its stems are very thorny. It needs little or no pruning and is generally a trouble-free rose that's extremely easy to grow. DIRECTORY p143

roses for ground cover

Ground-cover roses provide excellent value for money. They'll cover ground, prevent weeds from emerging and provide a carpet of colour throughout the summer months.

Kent

Kent is one of a group of roses known as the County Series, which includes other roses such as Suffolk, Wiltshire and Berkshire. Kent stands out from the crowd though, as a ground-cover rose. Bred by Poulsen of Denmark in 1988, it really is exceptionally good and of very high quality. In the early 1990s, it won many awards which highlighted the fact that a ground-cover rose could hold its own among all the other roses being introduced at that time. The flowers are small and semi-double to double, and are a brilliant pure white. It repeat-flowers very well, with flowers continuing throughout the summer. The scent is light and musky and the foliage is small, dark and a glossy green. These dark leaves make a wonderful backdrop to the purity of the white flowers. Kent looks absolutely fantastic planted en masse and I know several landscapers who use it as ground cover on banks. It's also a super rose for growing in containers and could even be trained to trail over a balcony. It's worthwhile trying other roses from the County Series as they come in a range of colours from cherry-red to soft pink and even bright yellow. They're all exceptionally good but Kent is my choice for its elegant, long-lasting display. DIRECTORY p136

Aviateur Blériot

I'm experimenting with this rose as ground cover, pegging it down so that it covers a gentle slope. It's an exceptionally beautiful rambling rose, first introduced in the 1900s. It was extremely popular on its introduction but, sadly, it's not widely seen today although it is available from some specialist rose nurseries. The flowers are absolutely gorgeous. They open from apricot buds which gently and softly fade from yellow through to cream and white. The flowers are double and have a good scent which I've heard described as being similar to magnolias. It's a very vigorous grower with an exceptionally long flowering season and, grown on a wall, it can make a big, imposing plant. As a ground cover, I'm planning to keep it within the limits of the large area I've provided for it. It's sometimes seen in public gardens in Europe, grown as a weeping standard, where it makes a very romantic-looking, exceptionally beautiful display. The foliage is particularly healthy and dark green, acting as a very good backdrop to the pale flowers. It's well worth making the effort to secure this rambler, whether you decide to grow it on a wall or experiment with it as ground cover. You might like to try planting it close to a doorway – somewhere you pass regularly – so you can enjoy its scent and old-world quality. DIRECTORY p155

Ballerina

This very pretty Hybrid Musk from the 1930s is a little
gem, absolutely smothering itself in clusters of small, musk-
scented flowers. The buds are rich and dark pink and open
to reveal single white-centred flowers which are edged in
deeper pink, fading to paler pink with age. The stamens
add a central splash of gold to each flower. The flowers
are produced in large trusses and are followed, if they're
not deadheaded, by small orange hips. 'Ballerina' is a
reliable rose with strong, healthy growth. If you're looking
for a low-growing, low-spreading rose you'll find it an
excellent choice. I've seen it grown as a ground cover to
great effect at St. Anne's Rose Garden, Raheny, Co.
Dublin and have also seen it growing on banks where it
has been allowed to trail. In addition, it makes a very
successful container plant and it can also can be grown
as a short standard, where it makes a neat and tidy
display. It's happy to grow in sun or part-shade which it
particularly appreciates in warmer climates, where it
holds its flower colour for much longer. DIRECTORY p145

The Countryman

The Countryman is a relatively new variety, having been
introduced by David Austin in the late 1980s, but it's one
with all the characteristics of an old-fashioned rose. The
flowers are fully double and open a rich, deep, glowing
pink, gradually fading to a soft old-rose colour. They
appear in clusters of between three and seven. The foliage
is very healthy and dark green and the stems are thorny.
It has an upright habit but the stems can sometimes flop
at the top, especially in warm climates, where it can grow
over two metres high. The great characteristic of The
Countryman is that its growth is always wider than it is
tall. The fragrance of the flowers is also very good – it's a
rich, old-rose fragrance overlaid with a scent of ripe
strawberries. It can be used as ground cover but it will be
necessary to peg the growths down to train them along
the ground, and it's important to prepare the soil well in
advance. Given rich growing conditions, it will make a
good, full plant. By planting it in groups, you'll get a
stunning display when it's in full flower. DIRECTORY p149

Nozomi

This is a charming rose of great character. The flowers are single and small and a beautiful shell-pink and the petals have a mother-of-pearl-like quality. In full flower, it's a very beautiful rose, resembling a burst of apple blossom. 'Nozomi' was produced in Japan in the late 1960s where it was grown as a miniature climbing rose, but in Europe it's used as ground cover. The quality of its coverage can be improved by pegging down the stems, which helps it to spread further. 'Nozomi' is also very attractive used in large rock gardens, where its stems can be used to trail over the rocks and I've also seen it growing very effectively in containers, where its trailing habit is again very pleasing. Sadly, it only flowers once in the season but it's really beautiful when it does. Occasionally, especially if it's in a warm, sunny position, it will produce small red rosehips. It has good disease-resistance and the tiny foliage is a glossy green. DIRECTORY p144

roses for
small gardens

This is a selection of neat and tidy roses which are
ideal for growing in restricted spaces.

Iceberg

What an iconic rose! It has to be among the most
popular of Floribunda roses grown in gardens
today. If you see it flowering en masse you'll be
overwhelmed by its sheer elegance. The double
flowers are pure brilliant white and it flowers
continuously from early summer until well into
autumn. The scent is light and soft – faintly
reminiscent of lily-of-the-valley. It's generally
disease-resistant and the foliage is a rich, dark
green, acting as a superb backdrop to the
startling white flowers. It responds well to good
soil and careful pruning. It's better to prune
lightly, as hard pruning sacrifices flower. There is
also a magnificent climbing version. If you can
give Iceberg some room, it's worthwhile planting
it in blocks, so you can really appreciate the
fullness of its superb display. To squeeze in even
three plants in the smallest garden will make a
big difference. I grow it in my own garden
underplanted with white variegated hostas and
Alchemilla mollis, which together provide a froth
of lime and olive-green. It also makes an excellent
cut flower, as it lasts a long time in water. I can't
recommend this rose highly enough. There are
fantastic displays of it in Pierre Bergé's garden in
Provence and also in the Cellars-Hohenort Hotel,
South Africa, where the walls of the building are
whitewashed. The combined effect is light and
airy, with a refreshing feel. DIRECTORY p130

Arthur Bell

'Arthur Bell' is an excellent rose for a small garden. It helps to brighten up shady areas, as its lovely rich colour adds a touch of sunlight to what might otherwise be a dull spot. It was raised by McGredy in Northern Ireland in the mid 1960s, and is as popular today as it was on its release. The scent is absolutely delicious – fruity, rich and strong – and the colour is best described as a deep golden yellow, gradually fading to primrose and lemon. It's especially useful in yellow and orange planting schemes. Its flowers are produced in medium-sized clusters. 'Arthur Bell' also makes an excellent cut flower and rain is never a problem, as the flowers stand up extremely well to damp and even stormy weather. A number of years ago I saw a magnificent display of this rose growing in Sir Thomas and Lady Dixon Park in Belfast, an exceptional rose garden run by Belfast City Council. It's a garden I always enjoy visiting, since you're sure to see the best of the best roses there.

DIRECTORY p131

Korresia

Floribunda roses make an excellent choice for small gardens. I'm always attracted to the yellow ones; there are so many reds and pinks to choose from and I believe the yellow ones add an extra splash of valuable colour. 'Korresia' is one Floribunda that stands out. Dating from the 1970s, it's been used as a bedding rose for many years. It's a very healthy, fully double, pure golden-yellow cultivar. The bush is compact in its growth, with light green, glossy foliage, and the flowers have a rich, sweet scent. These flowers are borne in clusters of between three and seven. The plant is exceptionally free-flowering and repeats really well. It's also very tolerant of rain and is happy whether grown in hot or cool climates, rich or poor soil. What is more, it makes an excellent cut flower, as the blooms last a long time in water and hold well before dropping their petals. 'Korresia' can be grown singly, but I always think it looks best in a small group. I often use it with differently shaped flowers and mixed colours, such as salvias and blue and purple flowers, where the contrasting tones make for a rich display. It works equally well with flowers of complimentary shades and tones such as *Allium obliquum,* seen here. Often sold under the name of 'Friesia', this award-winning rose is regarded as one of the very best yellow Floribundas. DIRECTORY p131

Belle de Crécy

This is one of the most popular Gallica roses, introduced in the late 1820s. If you appreciate roses with unusual colouring, the subtle colour changes of the flowers of 'Belle de Crécy' set it apart from many others. The colour starts with the rich crimson buds, but these open to cerise, deep pink, magenta, lilac, mauve, and even tints of grey. It's a stunning concoction. What's more, each flower encapsulates its own world of colour, as the colours change from the centre of the flower to the edge of each petal. The fully double flowers are produced singly or in small clusters. They have an old-fashioned shape and are roughly quartered with a mass of small petals. These are pleated and quilled around a central green eye. Mildew can be a problem, so it's important to provide a sunny, open position where there is plenty of air circulation. The scent is strong and sweet – typical of an old rose. 'Belle de Crécy' is ideal as a specimen in a small garden where you can really appreciate the ever-changing moods, charm and subtlety of its ravishing colour tones, as well as its exceptional scent. DIRECTORY p143

Dainty Bess

Single roses were popular in the 1920s and 'Dainty Bess' is one which is still grown today, which, I believe, says a lot about the charm and quality of its flowers. It's a real classic – one of the most beautiful single pink roses I know. The flowers appear in clusters of three to five and are pale pink. The petals have wavy edges. The beauty and simplicity of this rose is enhanced by the purple filaments. It's these that make it sublime. 'Dainty Bess' blooms continuously throughout the season and the flowers are particularly beautiful when the sunlight catches them from behind. The growth is light, which adds to the unfussy effect this plant brings to the garden, and the scent is light and fruity. If you're looking for a rose with great charm, and one that has its own special character, you'll find it all in 'Dainty Bess.' There is also a climbing version that was introduced in 1935 in America. It also repeat-flowers well and can reach a height of three metres. The first flowering of this climber is always exceptional, after which you can expect intermittent flushes throughout the flowering season. DIRECTORY p134

Mevrouw Nathalie Nypels

This is a superb compact rose that gives a great display. Its beauty lies in its tidy, bushy habit and its willingness to flower. The flowers start a salmon to rich pink and gradually pale through every shade of pink until each one turns white. The result of having some flowers opening and others fading at any one time gives an apple-blossom-like effect which is really stunning. This rose bears a great profusion of flowers in clusters, sometimes with as many as fifteen flowers per cluster. The foliage is dark green and glossy, and healthy, too. It's also a rose to be recommended because of its long flowering period; it starts in May and only stops in winter when the weather reaches its coldest. Careful attention to deadheading makes a difference in prolonging the display. It's an easy rose to propagate; cuttings root readily. If you want a low-growing rose that really pays for itself, you'll find it hard to match 'Mevrouw Nathalie Nypels'. It looks fabulous used to border a path, which has been done to great effect in many public gardens, but it's also a super rose for growing in a small garden where space may be limited. You can expect a fabulous display from just one plant.

DIRECTORY p152

roses for balconies and roof gardens

If you garden on a balcony or roof garden, here is a selection of roses that are ideally suited to growing in containers in these conditions. They'll provide a colourful display all summer long.

Abraham Darby

This is one of the first David Austin roses that I truly fell in love with, thanks to its combination of unusual colouring and delicious scent. It's one of the larger flowering English roses and I was fascinated to hear that in David Austin's breeding of this rose, there was no old-rose element. The flowers are generous and cup-shaped. I find the colour particularly attractive; the dominant shade is pink but, when you look closely, you can see a mixture of yellow, soft orange and peach underlying the pink. The outer petals fade to a soft yellow towards the edges. I've grown Abraham Darby in several gardens and find that it responds well to feeding and enjoys good soil. In one area where the soil was poor, the rose didn't perform and quickly succumbed to disease, so my advice is, feed this beauty generously and you'll be rewarded. The fragrance is another of its stunning features – a typical rose scent, high in fruity tones. Raspberries and pears come to mind. If you grow Abraham Darby in a container on a balcony or roof garden, you'll be able to appreciate this magnificent scent at close quarters. The container should be as large as you can accommodate.

DIRECTORY p139

Général Schablikine

I've always adored this rose. Its unique colouring is a magnificent blend of copper, coral and cherry-red that always draws the eye. The silky petals have a shimmering quality, which I believe also influences the colour. This is a Tea rose with a light to medium-sweet, tea-like fragrance, particularly in the early afternoon, that is slightly reminiscent of Earl Grey tea. The blooms have an especially beautiful shape, particularly as they open, and they also have a lovely nodding quality. The new growth is plum-coloured. Though 'Général Schablikine' is generally grown as a bush, it can also be grown as a climber against a wall where the very profuse flowers can really be appreciated. It's hardly ever out of bloom and so appreciates rich growing conditions. In fact, I would call this a greedy rose that really enjoys good feeding. If you're going to grow it in a container on a terrace or balcony, use the best-quality compost you can find and give it regular liquid feeding once it's established. Then you'll find it grows quite vigorously. With sun and shelter, and the right soil conditions, this rose is truly exceptional, with both compact growth and healthy foliage. DIRECTORY p157

Fantin-Latour

For those of you who are familiar with the work of the artist Fantin-Latour, this rose is a fitting tribute. I have fond memories of visiting the National Gallery of Ireland in Dublin where there is a stunning painting by this artist of an old-fashioned double rose. It could easily be the rose named after him; the picture captures the essence of its beauty. 'Fantin-Latour' is sometimes classified among the Centifolias, though it is a modern hybrid. The rose produces clusters of flowers and is only once-flowering, blooming through the month of June. The buds open to quartered rosettes with a button eye at the centre and the flowers are a good rose-pink, massed with petals. As the flowers fade, they take on flesh-pink tones. 'Fantin-Latour' is fast-growing and can reach four metres in height if grown against a wall. By training the branches horizontally, you will encourage more flowers to break from lateral shoots, which will add to the overall effect when the rose is in full bloom. This rose is extremely popular and widely available, and it has a sweet, delicate scent. It's definitely worth trying it on a roof garden or balcony, but make sure that the pot is sufficiently large to enhance the fullness of this gorgeous rose. DIRECTORY p146

Madame Louis Lévêque

When you're selecting a rose for a roof garden or balcony it's not usual to select an old-fashioned variety as your first choice. However, the Moss rose 'Madame Louis Lévêque' is excellent, as it really enjoys the sort of warm, sheltered spot that can often be provided on a balcony. Of course, it's also a great garden plant and I recommend it for a large container which can be positioned anywhere in the garden where you can give it the shelter that it enjoys. Its growth is upright and the foliage is long and pointed. It does have moss on the buds but this isn't as strong as on other varieties. Its flowers are large and flamboyant. Sadly, in wet weather, they're inclined to ball but if the plant is given sunshine and shelter, they open to large, globular flowers in a glorious shade of soft, pale pink. The fragrance is strong and quite pronounced. If you grow it in the garden, I find that it's best positioned in a mixed border, where it's easy to disguise the lower part of the plant, as this can be a little bit leggy. This rose looks stunning when combined with cottage-garden perennials such as *Nepeta*. It does repeat-flower but only lightly through the season.

DIRECTORY p147

Souvenir d'Adolphe Turc

This is a Polyantha from the 1920s that has stood the test of time. The flower colour is a palest coral, which changes gradually to pink of varying shades. The colour is more intense in cool climates, while in warmer regions, it may become a little washed out. The flowers have a light, musky scent. They expose their centres and are semi-double, produced in large clusters of up to thirty. The flowers weigh heavily on the stems, causing them to arch, but it still keeps a neat shape. The foliage is light and pale green and there are very few thorns. This is a super rose for growing in containers on balconies or roof gardens; its compact habit creates the ideal shape for a large pot or tub. It's best to give it a pot all to itself. Liquid feeding little and often is the trick for keeping it healthy once it has established. This rose may be difficult to find, more so in the UK than in the rest of Europe, but it's worth seeking it out. Specialist rose nurseries should be able to help. The soft pink colouring of 'Souvenir d'Adolphe Turc' is so easy to combine with other plants and it's a joy to see it in full flower. DIRECTORY p149

roses as cut flowers

Roses make one of the most beautiful cut flowers. This selection is especially suited to lasting well in water. Many have superb fragrance which adds to their appeal.

Just Joey

This rose is a great favourite of mine and has won countless awards over the years. I always plant it, as it does astonishingly well in Irish weather conditions, never really being affected by rain. What makes this rose special is its wonderful blousy flowers, which are an apricot-copper colour. The buds are beautifully shaped and open to wavy petals. The flowers are large and, as they mature, other complementary tones appear, such as buff, cream and orange, but the undersides of the petals always remain a rich apricot. These combine beautifully with the copper-tinted new foliage that develops around the flowers. The effect is quite stunning when you see a plant with flowers at different stages; it's a mix of all of these colours. The fragrance is medium and sweet. 'Just Joey' makes a splendid cut flower which lasts well in water. It's best planted in a group of a minimum of three to get the best effect and to provide enough flowers for cutting without depleting its garden display. I've always admired the magnificent display of this rose at St. Anne's Rose Garden near Clontarf in Dublin where you can see it planted en masse and get the full benefit of the foliage and flowers. DIRECTORY p132

Ingrid Bergman

If you're looking for one rose to grow
specially for cutting, you'll find it hard to
beat the award-winning Ingrid Bergman. It
really is one of the best red roses to use as
a cut flower. It's got everything – colour,
shape, fragrance and perfect long stems.
It's a stunning velvety rose with a medium-
to-sweet scent. The buds are perfectly
shaped and are almost black before they
open. The petals of the opening blooms
curl outwards giving a full, luscious effect.
It flowers each summer from June and
repeats well until the first frosts come in
late autumn. It lasts well in water, stands
up well to rain, and is a strong, vigorous
and compact plant with good disease-
resistance. There's a large planting of
Ingrid Bergman in a garden in south Co.
Dublin that I've been watching for the last
ten or twelve years. About thirty plants are
grown in a block along a white-painted
wall. The contrast between the white wall,
the dark green foliage and the rich red
flowers is quite spectacular. It's a display
that never fails to deliver. DIRECTORY p132

Mammy Blue

I've only grown this rose in the past few years, my curiosity having been fired by reading many descriptions of its unusual colouring and beautiful scent. It was bred by the French rose company, Delbard, producers of some of the finest modern roses in France. Both the colour and scent lived up to expectations in my own garden. The colour is an unusual bluish mauve – the colour of lilac – which should be a fantastic hit with flower arrangers, as it's so special. Its blooms have pointed centres and recurving petals; they're a perfect Hybrid Tea shape. The scent is superb; close your eyes and imagine honey, violets, vanilla, burnt sugar, lemons and a hint of geranium, and you're not even coming close to the complex fragrance of this magnificent rose. It responds well to a sunny, sheltered spot and needs a light annual prune. The stems are far from heavy so I suggest planting it in groups for greatest impact. I have found it to be disease-resistant. It also appreciates good feeding and I recommend the use of a mulch to keep in moisture during the summer. It may take a season to settle in but, once established, the plant is attractive, neat and upright. DIRECTORY p134

Eglantyne

Named after Eglantyne Jebb, the woman who founded the Save The Children Fund, this is a gorgeous rose with old-rose charm and an old-rose fragrance to match. I think it's one of David Austin's prettiest English roses. The flowers are a mid-to-soft pink, with deeper shading on the back of the petals, and as the flowers open fully, the pink colour becomes light and delicate. The flower shape is truly old-fashioned with a centre made up of a mass of quilled petals. Eglantyne makes an upright, medium-height bushy plant that becomes very twiggy. It blooms continuously throughout the entire season and the flower fragrance is strong and sweet. It can be prone to blackspot, so good cultivation is needed, and it appreciates a rich soil in an open, bright position. As with many David Austin roses, it makes a great display when planted in a group and can add real old-world charm to a mixed border. It also makes a stunning cut flower – it's one of those gorgeous roses that looks luxurious when you have filled a bowl with nothing else. DIRECTORY p145

Pierre de Ronsard (Eden Rose 88)

This is one of my favourite roses and would rank even higher on my list if it had a scent. For me, this is its only drawback – you would expect something so beautiful to have a perfume to match. Even so, the quality, shape and colouring of its flowers are exquisite and I'm always captured by the stunning beauty of this truly eye-catching rose. It has an old-fashioned character with delicate colouring – warm, glowing pink in the centre of the flower fading to soft, creamy pink on the outer petals. The flowers are large, very full and double, and cup-shaped. They are slow to unfold from bud and they last well on the plant. They also last well in water, which makes them excellent cut flowers. Some catalogues describe the rose as scented but I have never got a scent, either growing it in my own garden or examining it closely in others, and I always think this is a pity. It's a climbing rose that's compact in its growth and when it settles in, it's very vigorous. However, it's inclined to take its time – in some cases it's been three years before I've started to reap the rewards. It only has a few thorns and, when established, the flowers are very abundant with the advantage that they appear from the top of the plant downwards. Add to all this the fact that it flowers continuously, and you'll see why I recommend it. DIRECTORY p163

roses in contemporary gardens

Roses have a place in modern garden design. They offer value with their long-lasting displays. Here is a selection that are especially suited to contemporary gardens.

Graham Thomas

If I were allowed take only one rose to a desert island, of course I'd be spoiled for choice, but Graham Thomas would be high on my list. It's possibly the best-known of all of David Austin's roses, and rightly so. Named in honour of the great rosarian Graham Stuart Thomas, who did more than anyone else to popularise old-fashioned roses, it's fitting that such a fantastic rose should carry his name. If ever there was a contemporary rose that fitted modern gardens and modern garden design, this is it. I've seen it used to great effect; planted in large groups, it simply steals the show. What makes this rose so special is the richness of its golden-yellow flowers and their delicious sweet fragrance, which has been described as a 'fresh tea fragrance', with 'a cool violet' character. It's quite complex, with lots of ripe fruit scents hidden in there, too. The growth of Graham Thomas is upright – it can also be grown as a climbing rose where it can reach at least three metres – and the foliage is attractive. It flowers repeatedly from early summer until late autumn and is also fantastic as a cut flower. If you're looking for a golden-yellow rose with old-fashioned character that still manages to works well in a contemporary garden, Graham Thomas is hard to beat. DIRECTORY p138

Dioressence

This beautiful French Hybrid Tea is noted for its exceptionally sweetly scented flowers that smell of citrus mixed with moss and geranium. They are also a very special colour; the buds have a bluish-lilac tinge and when they open, they are a combination of pink and lilac – a wonderful colour for flower arranging. The colouring also makes it ideal for planting in modern gardens, as it can add a sophisticated, contemporary touch to planting schemes. 'Dioressence' looks best planted in groups of three or five and I have recently seen it in a mixed border combined with perennials of similar colouring, including salvias. The effect was magical. The company Delbard, which produced this rose, offers an extensive range of new roses every year and I'm delighted to see that they put great emphasis on fragrance. 'Dioressence' is a fine example of their breeding programme. Many of Delbard's roses are happiest in warm, sheltered, sunny spots and though the quality of their flowers is superb, I have found that they're not always at home in the moist, damp, Irish climate of my own garden. If you want to get the best from 'Dioressence', careful positioning, good drainage and sunshine are essential. DIRECTORY p134

Blush Rambler

A rambling rose that was extremely popular in Edwardian days, 'Blush Rambler' was often seen growing around cottages. What a pity it's not seen so much today, as I believe it would fit in so well with many contemporary plantings. It has grace and style, and when it's mature and established and in full flower, it is a striking sight. The branches are vigorous but there are hardly any thorns, which makes it a very useful choice where there'll be people passing by. The flowers are semi-double, opening bright pink and fading to a light, almost white colour. They are produced in fantastic clusters of anything between twenty and fifty flowers. The fragrance is delicious. 'Blush Rambler' is extremely happy in a warm, sheltered spot, and does exceptionally well in warmer gardens than my own here in Ireland. Sadly, its petals can be marked slightly by heavy rain. Despite it being an old rose, if you have a modern garden and can allow it the space to grow, it's worth searching for. DIRECTORY p160

Anna Livia

Anna Livia has become a popular rose for contemporary planting. It's often used in modern public planting schemes, where its showy display adds vibrancy and colour through the summer months. In 1988 it was presented to the City of Dublin as a gift from Kordes, a German rose nursery, to commemorate the city's millennium celebrations. Since then it has become a popular choice in Irish gardens. Its name refers to the river Liffey that flows through the centre of Dublin. The flowers are an attractive shape and a lovely rich salmon-pink colour. This colouring fades gently towards the centre of the flower, which opens to a semi-double, exposing the central stamens. The petals are marked by rain and this can give the flowers a red tinge, but this somehow doesn't seem to detract from the colouring. In fact, in many ways it enhances and deepens it. The flowers of Anna Livia appear in large clusters of up to fifteen, it has long thorns and dark green leaves. It can be susceptible to blackspot. For best impact, this rose should be planted in a group of at least three plants.

DIRECTORY p135

Morning Jewel

This climbing rose is popular in Germany, where it is much loved, though it was originally raised in Scotland. It gives a great show right through the summer, a fact which means that it offers really good value for the space it takes up, especially in modern gardens where space is at a premium. The double flowers stand up to wet weather extremely well and are a rich, luminous pink. I think this colour looks very modern and believe it will add a fashionable splash of colour to even the smallest of gardens. The flowers are produced on single stems or in clusters with up to half a dozen flowers to a cluster. They have a pleasant, medium-sweet fragrance. I've seen 'Morning Jewel' growing against the sunny gable end of a modern town house. The wall was painted a delicate shade of pink and the harmony between the rich pink flowers of 'Morning Jewel' and the painted wall was gentle yet striking.

DIRECTORY p164

roses for cottage gardens

These are roses that have an old-world charm. They are especially suitable if you are after a cottage-garden look. They will complement other cottage garden flowers to bring to life a traditional style.

Madame Hardy

When I think of an old-fashioned white rose, it's usually 'Madame Hardy' that comes to mind. It's truly exquisite. In the world of old roses, it's iconic and is definitely one of the most desirable and treasured of old white roses. Very popular in Ireland, where it has always been appreciated and loved, it can be seen growing in many old-fashioned gardens from north to south. I think, due to the ease with which it can be propagated, it has been spread as cuttings. I even know of one village in Donegal where it can be seen in several gardens, having been passed from one neighbour to another. That's one of the beauties of growing a treasured plant like 'Madame Hardy'. The flowers are fully double and are quite big, considering the number that are produced. At the centre of the flower is a green eye which I adore. It adds a magical quality to each bloom, making them look elegant and sumptuous. The scent is strong, gloriously sweet and quite pronounced. The growth is strong and upright and the foliage is a bright, fresh green that looks especially good when young. I've grown 'Madame Hardy' both as a specimen plant and in mixed borders, where it associates extraordinarily well with perennials, such as geraniums, and other cottage-garden flowers. Of all the old roses I grow, this ranks among the best double whites. DIRECTORY p136

Crown Princess Margareta

David Austin produces a huge range of English roses, the majority of which are ideally suited to any cottage garden, hence I find it difficult to choose one rather than another for this section of the book. Crown Princess Margareta wins because of its exceptional colouring; it's a lovely apricot to gold, darker in the centre and fading towards the edges. The flowers are full and the petals quilled. In cooler gardens, the colour can be a little more intense, especially in the centre of the flower where more copper tones shine through. The flowers sometimes appear singly and sometime in clusters and have a strong, fruity scent. The bush makes an attractive rounded, arching shape, which shows the flowers off well. The leaves are dark green and are generally healthy. In warmer countries, Crown Princess Margareta can be grown as a pillar rose, but in the colder gardens of the north it's best grown as a shrub. As with many of David Austin's roses, I believe that, for the greatest impact, it's best planted in groups of uneven numbers – three or five, if space allows. This adds to the overall effect, bringing a fullness and opulence to the display when the rose is in full bloom.

DIRECTORY p136

Gloire de Dijon

This hardy Tea rose falls into my
'greedy-rose category' in that it needs to
be fed well to do well. You rarely find it
doing just OK; it's either very poor or
fabulous and never seems to be in
between. This, I'm sure, is due to how
it's been cultivated. But let me start by
telling you that the fully double flower
shape is truly exquisite. It's the
quintessential cottage-garden rose, the
one you'd expect to find growing over
the door of every thatched cottage. The
flower colour is divine; if you can
imagine buff, fawn, yellow, and honey
tones all blending together, I think
you'll get the picture. There's a real
warmth and character about it. The
strong tea-like fragrance is sweet and
the perfume will carry on a gentle
summer breeze. But now to return to its
cultivation: to get the very best from
this climbing rose you need to prepare
the soil in advance of planting. Plenty
of organic matter and occasional
helpings of rose feed will help to keep it
at its best, while it only needs light
pruning. There's a magnificent specimen
of 'Gloire de Dijon' at Altamont
Gardens near Tullow, Co. Carlow.
Every time I see it, it takes my breath
away. Overall, it's a truly iconic rose.

DIRECTORY p157

Awakening (Probuzeni)

Awakening originated in Czechoslovakia in 1935 as a sport of one of my favourite roses, 'New Dawn'. In Czechoslovakia it's listed under the name 'Probuzeni'. It can be obtained from specialist rose growers but I'll never understand why this hardy, vigorous-growing rambler with a long flowering period isn't more widely available in garden centres. It's simply a double-flowered version of 'New Dawn'. Each flower is fully double and the colour at the centre of the flower is a pinkish apricot, gradually fading towards the outer petals, which have a silver-pink

quality. It's the combination of these colours with the fullness of the flower that adds up to the voluptuous effect. I love the way the individual flowers are quartered, and the central petals are often quilled. In full flower, Awakening is one of the most sublime of roses. The flowers can be damaged by rain, which can leave marks on the petals, but despite this, the floral effect is superb. Awakening is noted for its exceptional hardiness and this has made it a popular choice on continental Europe. I've seen it growing on the walls of whitewashed cottages where it contributed greatly to that archetypal chocolate-box look. DIRECTORY p161

Stanwell Perpetual

In many ways, old roses are like people; they all have their own individual characters. Some are showy and blousy, others are elegant and refined. This is one of the things that I enjoy about owning a varied collection of these roses. One favourite, though somewhat delicate, is 'Stanwell Perpetual'. It's been around since the 1830s, so it's fair to say it has stood the test of time. There's a great elegance and beauty about it. The flowers are a delicate blush-pink, fading as they age to near-white. They are attractively shaped and usually carried on extremely thorny short stems. I suppose one of the things that I enjoy most about this rose is the fact that, unusually for an old rose, it flowers continuously, starting in early summer and going on all the way into early winter. It's a rose that's very tolerant of poor soil conditions, which has to be a plus, but it does take time to settle in. The stems are long and arching, which adds to the character and generally open and airy shape of the plant. I find that 'Stanwell Perpetual' makes a wonderful cottage-garden rose, as it mixes so well with many other plants, including perennials. DIRECTORY p148

Ispahan

Here is one of the world's greatest Damask roses, a true beauty which looks stunning grown either in a cottage garden or in a formal planting at a great house. I've even seen it used as a hedge, where its great profusion of flower created a memorable sight. 'Ispahan' is truly in a class all of its own, ranking among the very best of the once-flowering, old-fashioned roses. If you're looking for such a rose with character and good qualities, then this should be high on your list. It's blessed with an exquisite fragrance that is sweet and pronounced and that amply matches the quality of its flowers. These appear in clusters and are a rich, mid-pink with a slight lilac tinge. I love their central button eye. The flowers are not as large as those of other Damask roses, but 'Ispahan' makes up for this by having a longer flowering period than most. Despite being once-flowering, it continues flowering week after week for over six weeks, making it one of the longest-flowering Damask roses. 'Ispahan' is one of my favourites, especially for its delicious scent. I can fairly say it's a rose that I couldn't bear to be without.

DIRECTORY p150

roses for autumn and winter interest

These roses help to continue garden interest after the flowers have faded. Their berries and hips add a magical look to our gardens when little else is showing.

Penelope

This is a fabulous rose, producing semi-double, palest creamy pink flowers with a rich musky fragrance. It is considered to be one of the best of the Hybrid Musks and is widely grown. The back of each petal is a lovely dark peach pink, opening to expose yellow stamens at the centre of the flower. In full bloom, these flowers glow in a creamy, buttery pink shade. The flowers are loosely produced in clusters numbering from six to twelve. It produces a particularly good flush in early summer and can be rather shy in autumn, so it is essential that you deadhead if you want to continue the flowering late into the season. The hips are good in winter, being small and rich red, but you will have to choose between late flowers and hips as you can't have both. This is a favourite rose and one I always enjoy in full flower. 'Penelope', like so many other Hybrid Musks, can be used to make a hedge. I have seen it grown on a low bank in a garden in Donegal where it stretched for about twenty feet, making an informal hedge that gently trailed over the bank. In full flower, this was a fantastic sight. Strolling along the path beside it, you could really enjoy its scent. DIRECTORY p137

Bobbie James

'Bobbie James' is a rose I can rate very highly on many counts. In my opinion, it's one of the best small-flowered ramblers you can grow. It was discovered as a seedling by the late Graham Stuart Thomas, who was responsible for popularising and saving so many old-fashioned roses. The flowers are semi-double with that lovely cherry-blossom quality and they're produced in fantastic profusion in huge clusters. The flower is white and, on opening, golden stamens are exposed in the centre. If the flowers aren't removed, you'll get lovely red-orange rosehips from autumn into winter, thus extending the season with extra interest. I love to see rosehips in the winter garden; they're a part of the rose that's often neglected, but I think they have a beauty and charm all of their own. The scent of 'Bobbie James' is a very strong musk and is pleasing when caught on the summer breeze. It's a rose that I can recommend for growing through large trees or an old apple tree. That way you can really appreciate the hanging clusters of flowers. I've also seen it allowed to ramble through a dividing hedge in a large garden. As well as being great for autumn and winter interest, I think this rose, which first appeared in the 1960s, has a place in contemporary garden design. It's time to give 'Bobbie James' a new lease of life and plant it in new and interesting ways.

DIRECTORY p154

Fritz Nobis

'Fritz Nobis' makes a very bushy, dense shrub. Produced in Germany in the 1940s, it's still extremely valuable today. I'm particularly fond of it when it's in bud, as these have a really beautiful shape, not unlike the Hybrid Tea 'Ophelia'. The flowers are a medium-pink with pale salmon tones and they appear in long-stemmed clusters. When fully open, they reveal a centre of golden-yellow stamens. The foliage is glossy and dark green and the growth zigzags. The fragrance is delicious, strong, sweet and spicy – reminiscent of cloves. 'Fritz Nobis' is a very hardy rose which is really well suited to cold areas. It can be susceptible to blackspot but, with good cultivation, this can be overcome. The flowers are excellent for cutting, but if they're left on, they're often followed by round, dull, reddish-orange rosehips that add an attractive touch to the winter garden. I've often used this rose at the back of a mixed border where, planted in groups, it really adds an elegant and charming summery touch. Late-flowering clematis are planted nearby, among them several of the viticella hybrids. One that associates extremely well is *Clematis* 'Flore Pleno'. The flowers are the colour of crushed raspberry coulis with a violet undertone, and they complement the flowers of 'Fritz Nobis' to perfection. DIRECTORY p146

Centenaire de Lourdes

This is an unusual French Floribunda from the 1950s that, sadly, isn't often seen in gardens. What a pity, as it's a real beauty. It produces abundant clusters of semi-double flowers which continue from early summer well into autumn. When the flowers open from deep pink buds they are a pale crimson colour. As they mature, they gradually fade to a mid-pink, especially towards the edges. The petals arc slightly wavy at the edges. The light scent is good and reminiscent of jasmine. The foliage has good disease-tolerance and the overall shape of the bush is rounded and tidy. For anyone interested in flower arranging, Centenaire de Lourdes is a super rose to use as a cut flower. It also provides marvellous clusters of rosehips that are orange in colour and add a splash to the autumn and winter garden. Like many of the older roses, I think it deserves a place in modern plantings and offers excellent value. Not only do you get the long flowering season, but also, when everything else is disappearing in the garden, you can really enjoy the colour of its rosehips. I would love to see this rose more widely grown.

DIRECTORY p135

curiosity roses

If you're looking for a more unusual rose, the following will provide you with a curiosity factor that will add that little something different to your garden.

Ash Wednesday (Aschermittwoch)

I had read about this rose for many years before growing it and was always fascinated by its name. I now grow it as a climber for its remarkable, if somewhat unusual, colouring which is like no other. From a distance the flowers have a curious soft grey appearance, but on closer inspection you'll discover that the unique colouring is a combination of the palest lilac and pink, with the reverse of the petals a silvery colour. I think the whole effect has best been described as a 'ghostly grey'. As the petals unfold, they create darker shadows that add to the ghostly effect. The flowers are very full and appear in clusters of anything between two and twelve flowers per cluster. Sadly, it only flowers once in the season but I look forward to its flowers like an old friend returning to my garden year after year. The growth is strong and vigorous, though it is slightly susceptible to blackspot, and the flower scent is medium to sweet. 'Ash Wednesday' also makes a superb cut flower, as its unusual colour can really be appreciated close up. It's a very special plant and one which should be more widely grown. If you're looking for a rose with a difference, I think this one will appeal. DIRECTORY p160

Bleu Magenta

This beautiful rambler is very special. I'm afraid its origins
are lost in obscurity but we do know that it was
introduced by a French nursery which popularised it in
the 1950s. It belongs to a group of what are sometimes
called 'blue' roses, though the colouring is actually a
shade of purple. In the case of 'Bleu Magenta', the
attractive flowers are a combination of crimson and rich
pink overlaid with purple. As the flowers mature, tones
of violet and slate-grey begin to emerge. Each flower is
fully double and they are borne in large clusters of up to
thirty flowers which, when in full bloom, are produced
in somewhat congested panicles. This rose has the great
advantage of not having any thorns. The scent is light
and if you close your eyes, you'll quickly detect floral
and grassy notes. 'Bleu Magenta' has the advantage of
flowering later in the season than many other roses.
There's a famous planting of this gorgeous rose at
Mottisfont Abbey, Hampshire, England, where it has
been combined with the beautiful, free-flowering pink
rose 'Debutante' to great effect. It also grows superbly at
Roseraie de l'Haÿ, one of France's most noted rose gardens.
DIRECTORY p160

Ferdinand Pichard

Here is a striped rose that always grabs people's attention
in my garden. Pale pink flowers, splashed and striped with
crimson, open from elegant buds. The markings are never
the same from flower to flower. These unusual blooms are
produced in clusters of three to five and, if well fed, it's
happy to produce many secondary flushes once the main
flowering has finished. The large, pale green foliage is
good and healthy, as is the rose as a whole, and it has
very thorny stems. The scent is a typical old-rose scent –
strong and sweet. 'Ferdinand Pichard' looks good when
planted in groups and associates well with other, richly
coloured roses. It's also very attractive as a cut flower.
When the flowers are in a vase, you can really appreciate
each one's intricate markings and curiously attractive
striping and splashing. If you grow it in warm climates, it
can reach up to three metres in height, but in cooler Irish
gardens it rarely exceeds a metre. This is a rose that has
great character and its curiously marked flowers will
always ensure it's in great demand. DIRECTORY p153

Variegata di Bologna

The curious colouring of this flower always attracts attention. It's a long-time favourite of mine and is certainly my preferred striped rose. 'Variegata di Bologna' originated in Italy as a sport of 'Victor Emmanuel' and was introduced to great acclaim in 1909. The flowers are voluptuous, opening from fat, rounded buds to beautiful, cup-shaped, fully double flowers which are quartered. The flowers are produced in clusters of between three and five blooms per cluster. The colouring is exquisite – pale rose-pink with crimson-purple stripes and splashes. As the flower matures, the pale pink background fades to near-white, which exaggerates the colour of the stripes. It always reminds me of raspberry ripple ice cream. It can be prone to balling in very wet weather and also sometimes gets blackspot, but don't let this dissuade you from growing this rose. It's a vigorous plant that appreciates deep, well-cultivated soil. The foliage is narrow and pointed. I've been told that it's a good rose to plant against a northwest-facing wall where it can enjoy a cool root run. Its old-rose fragrance is strong and sweet and gloriously heavy. The curious colouring of 'Variegata di Bologna' and its exotic name both contribute to its continuing popularity.

DIRECTORY p153

R. x odorata Viridiflora

This is possibly the most curiously coloured rose I grow and it's always a talking point when it's in flower. The buds are perfectly shaped and open to form small, attractive green flowers, though as they age, the flowers take on a rather untidy appearance. With maturity, comes brown markings, which make the flowers less attractive. There is no scent. If planted against a wall, it can reach a height of over two metres, but when grown as a freestanding bush, it usually reaches just over one metre in height. I know that, despite its lack of scent, it's popular with flower arrangers; it looks lovely in a vase with other roses, as well as other flowers. I suppose it's best described as a collector's rose – more of a novelty than a great beauty – but its curiosity value and unusual flowers have made it popular since the mid-1850s, and there are records of it being in cultivation as early as 1743. Its growth is similar to 'Old Blush' and it's thought that 'Viridiflora' is a sport of that rose. I've grown it against a north-facing wall for over twenty years where it happily produces flowers practically all year round.

DIRECTORY p153

roses for special occasions

If you're planning on celebrating a special occasion here's a selection of roses that you might like to consider giving as a gift or planting to mark the celebration.

Golden Celebration

This is a stunner. The only fault I can see is that the growth is gently arched and so the heavy flowers hang. Therefore, I recommend growing it as a low climber where I believe the flowers can be better appreciated. And let me tell you, the flowers are gorgeous so you'll want to see them to best advantage. The centre of each is a rich egg-yolk yellow (of course, I'm referring to free-range eggs!), the colour gently fading as the flower opens. The flowers are of great size yet never look clumsy, and the scent is well able to match the power, size and look of the flowers. When the flowers first open, they have a slight scent of tea, but as they develop further, other scents can be detected – crushed strawberries, ripe pears, and the delicious headiness of Sauternes wine. You'll be left confused as to whether you can drink or eat this beauty, or just look at it! Not surprisingly, this is a lovely rose to plant to mark a family celebration such as a golden wedding. A whole flowerbed full of this rose would look truly magnificent and would really show off its exceptional beauty and charm. You could also use it in a mixed border where it will associate very well with shades of blue and mauve. Its rich, yet soft yellow, colouring makes it the ideal partner for plants such as lavender, *Nepeta* and delphiniums. DIRECTORY p138

Warm Wishes

Since its introduction in 1994, Warm Wishes has become a very popular Hybrid Tea rose. It has won countless prizes all over the world for its vigour and excellent flower quality and its colour is a most attractive mixture of coral, apricot and pink. The colour gradually changes as the flower opens from its attractive, shapely buds. As the petals open, they gently curve back, producing a large, pointed blossom that is the perfect Hybrid Tea shape. The blooms are also highly scented, with a rich, fruity fragrance and they are produced on long stems which make them ideal for cutting, especially as they last well in water. This rose also has the quality of repeat-flowering quickly, so is noted for its long succession of flowers through the summer months. The foliage is dark green and very healthy. Warm Wishes is the ideal gift for most occasions. In the garden it makes a very attractive standard rose and I always think it looks fantastic when planted with other warm-coloured flowers such as day lilies, *Crocosmia* and apricot-tinted *Kniphofia*.

DIRECTORY p135

Blessings

'Blessings' is a bedding rose that could well be given as a gift in celebration of a birth or wedding. A Floribunda that was introduced in the late 1960s, it's a seedling of the famous rose 'Queen Elizabeth'. It's really exceptional for the sheer quantity of flower that it produces. These open from attractively shaped buds, which look like typical Hybrid Tea buds, but as they open fully, they taken on the much looser flower look that's a Floribunda characteristic. When fully open, the colour is a soft coral-pink. Though the shape of the flower isn't great, their exceptional colour and quantity make up for it. 'Blessings' starts flowering early in the season and continues well into late autumn, when you can expect a really good flush. The flowers are borne singly or in clusters and hold exceptionally well in rainy weather. The growth is vigorous and the leaves are large and dark green. It has excellent disease-resistance and is an extremely easy rose to grow. When planted in groups, it really looks superb and the impact of its numerous flowers will be multiplied.

DIRECTORY p134

Congratulations

Congratulations is an excellent long-stemmed rose to grow as a cut flower, as it lasts extremely well in water. With its medium to sweet fragrance, it's also a super rose to give to congratulate someone, whether for passing an exam, the birth of a baby or for moving into a new house. Introduced from Germany in 1979, it has become very popular in Europe and Australia, but doesn't seem to be widely available in the US at present. The flowers of Congratulations are very shapely, with a high centre, but they eventually open out completely. The colour is a rich pink that fades to a silvery pink as the flower opens. You will sometimes detect a soft yellow colour in the centre. Flowers are produced singly though occasionally you may get two or three on one stem, and the flowering is very abundant, continuing well into the autumn, usually until the first frost arrives. The plant has a slender, tall, upright growth, reaching over two metres when established, so it's also a good rose to use as a hedging plant. DIRECTORY p135

Ruby Wedding

If you have a ruby wedding to celebrate, this rose makes the perfect gift to honour forty years of marriage. It's a compact, extremely popular Hybrid Tea that's widely available in garden centres. The attractively shaped flowers are crimson in colour and open to a loosely formed double flower which is noted for holding its colour extremely well. It's usual for 'Ruby Wedding' to produce its flowers in clusters of up to five blooms. It's also continuous in its flowering, producing repeat flowers very quickly. The dark green, glossy foliage is particularly attractive and the new growth has a crimson tinge. The growth is vigorous and strong and it makes a dense, bushy plant, but blackspot can sometimes be a problem. 'Ruby Wedding' looks stunning either grown in a container or, as I have seen, planted towards the front of a fiery-coloured border. It's also a great choice for a small garden and the flowers are produced on strong stems, which also makes it ideal for cutting. DIRECTORY p133

directory

OPPOSITE: *R. xanthina* 'Canary Bird'

bush roses
HYBRID TEA, FLORIBUNDA

Bush roses are among the most versatile roses we can grow in our gardens. They are suitable for mass planting or they can be grown as groups in a mixed scheme. There is a huge variety and range to choose from. Many are richly scented and you will be spoiled for choice when it comes to selecting a colour.

Note on using the Directory

Rose classifications are explained in more detail in the Glossary (pages 182–183).

The date at the bottom of each entry tells you when the rose was introduced, and typical height (H) and spread (S) are also given.

Roses are arranged alphabetically within colour categories, by variety or species name.

Many roses change shade from bud to petal fall, but they have been arranged in the colour category that best describes the rose when in full flower.

More colour details are given within the descriptions.

Happy rose hunting!

white

ICEBERG
(see page 88)

This is one of the best Floribundas, providing a long display of semi-double white flowers with a light, soft scent. The foliage is rich and glossy green. It repeat-flowers well throughout the season and generally has good disease-resistance. It looks exceptionally well when planted in groups. In my opinion, this is one of the very best white roses you can grow. Iceberg benefits from being grown in an open, sunny position where the white flowers truly glisten. It should be sheltered from wind. The soil needs to be well-drained and the plant benefits from mulching and regular feeding.

Floribunda | 1958
H: 1m x S: 65cm

MARGARET MERRIL
(see page 70)

This is an extremely popular rose, and rightly so. Its flowers are very beautiful and it has an exquisite sweet scent. It's interesting to note that, in cool climates, the flowers take on a slight pink hue, whereas in very hot climates, they are purest white. Its only downfall is that it is prone to blackspot but, with good cultivation you should be able to overcome this. The dark green foliage is large and glossy. Margaret Merril requires light pruning. It's also important to deadhead this rose to ensure continued flowering, and it benefits from mulching and feeding.

Floribunda | 1977
H: 1.5m x S: 1m

PRISTINE

The blooms of this rose are exquisite and its award-winning scent superb. The centre of the flowers are a rich, creamy, ivory-white and as you move outwards, the edges of the petals take on a deeper tone and the overall colour becomes a pale blush-pink. It's also a very shapely rose with beautifully arranged petals whose edges are wavy and curl backwards.

This gives the flower great character. The flowers appear singly or in clusters of up to three or four. The foliage is dark green and is very disease-resistant. It's an excellent rose for cutting and also makes a super plant towards the back of a border, where it's best planted in a group of three or five.

Hybrid Tea | 1978
H: 1m x S: 80cm

soft yellow

PEACE

(syn. 'Madame A. Meilland')

Peace is one of the most widely grown roses in the world and is certainly one of the most famous. It produces large flowers that are dark yellow in the

centre, fading to pale yellow on the outer parts of the petals. The edges of the outermost petals are flushed pink and sometimes lined with red. It has a soft and subtle fragrance. The foliage is glossy and healthy and, though it has been superseded by other roses, it is still popular today. It's interesting to note that in all English-speaking countries it's called Peace – in 1945 it was presented to all the delegates at the formation of the United Nations. However, it's grown under different names around Europe; for example, in Italy it is known as 'Gioia' and in Germany 'Gloria Dei'.

Hybrid Tea | 1945
H: 1.5m x S: 1.25m

ARTHUR BELL

(see page 89)

An early-flowering Floribunda, this has bright and cheery flowers that open a deep golden yellow and gradually fade to a primrose and lemon mix. The scent is rich, fruity and strong. The leaves are dark green and glossy, and are generally healthy. There is a climbing sport which was introduced in 1978. It can grow to about three and a half metres in height with a two-metre spread. 'Arthur Bell' needs a sunny position and benefits from annual pruning. It has good disease-resistance and regular mulching and feeding can make a big difference to the quantity of flowers.

Floribunda | 1965
H: 1m x S: 80cm

KORRESIA

(see page 90)

This is a gorgeous, brilliant yellow Floribunda whose large, fully-double flowers have a strong, rich, rose scent. The foliage is light green and generally healthy. It repeat-flowers extremely well and should be lightly pruned when dormant. This rose prefers a sunny, open position and it's essential that the soil is well drained. It has excellent disease-resistance and benefits from regular feeding.

Floribunda | 1973
H: 75cm x S: 60cm

FREEDOM

A charming yellow rose and one that I'm very fond of. Although there are many yellow Hybrid Tea roses, this one has an exceptionally good rich colour and holds its colour really well. It's what I would describe as a true golden-yellow rose. It withstands wet weather and the flowers are carried on strong stems. The fragrance is light and sweet. Freedom looks fantastic when planted in large groups, where you can really appreciate the impact of its colour. I always find it benefits from a little extra feeding after its first flush of flowers.

Hybrid Tea | 1984
H: 80cm x S: 60cm

MRS OAKLEY FISHER

This is a single-flowering Hybrid Tea, a style of rose that was popular in the 1920s. I love the simplicity of

the flower and the central boss of crimson stamens and filaments contributes greatly to its charm. The colour is soft orange with copper tones, giving an apricot appearance overall. These colours pale towards the centre and become warmer towards the edges of the petals. The flowers close at night and reopen the following day. It's a healthy rose that produces rich green leaves. The thorns are large and the new growth is a coppery red that looks magnificent with the flowers.

Hybrid Tea | 1921
H: 1.5m x S: 1.25m

FELLOWSHIP (syn. Livin' Easy)

This is a very showy Floribunda. The petals of the brightly coloured flowers, which are orange to dark apricot, have a wavy quality. As the flowers age, the edges of the petals take on a crimson tone. The flowers are produced in clusters of three to seven.

The fragrance is light with a fruity sweetness and the plant produces healthy growth. There is a sport of this rose called Easy Going, produced in 1999. It's pale apricot with hints of pink. Both roses give a great display, especially with regular feeding and the application of an annual mulch.

Floribunda | 1992
H: 1m x S: 60cm

JUST JOEY
(see page 100)

This is an award-winning Hybrid Tea of great quality, recognised for its exceptionally good blooms. When the flowers are fully open, the petals have a lovely wavy quality. The colour is an attractive apricot-copper. It has a light scent and the foliage is dark green and healthy, with the new shoots having a copper-red tone. It makes a neat, bushy plant and is tolerant of disease.

Hybrid Tea | 1972
H: 1m x S: 75cm

ALEXANDER

This ranks as a truly eye-catching rose. It makes up for its lack of strong scent by being a sensational bright vermilion-red. I think it's one of the most vivid shades you'll find in a rose. Another good point is its strong growth and vigour. It quickly grows to at least two metres in height and carries a good crop of flowers on top of strong stems. To get the best from this rose, it will need good feeding. It makes an excellent cut flower. In general, the flowers are rain-resistant.

Hybrid Tea | 1972
H: 2m x S: 1.2m

INVINCIBLE

Though it's classified as a Floribunda, this gorgeous red rose has many Hybrid Teas in its parentage. The flowers are full with plenty of petals, so you'd be forgiven for thinking it's a Hybrid Tea. The flower colour is between a brilliant signal-red and blood-red and the flowers hold their colour well, right up to the point of petal fall. It contin-uously flowers throughout the summer and makes a very showy bedding  rose. The foliage is dark green, glossy and healthy and the scent is light and sweet. Invincible is a good strong grower and is really showy when planted in groups.

Floribunda | 1983
H: 1m x S: 75cm

Knock Out has taken America by storm. It has become one of the most popular roses there. It is celebrated for its hardiness and disease-resistance, producing clusters of what are described as 'fire-engine red' flowers. In hot climates, this colour changes to a lighter cherry-red. It has an exceptionally  long flowering period. The scent is light and reminiscent of tea. It makes a compact shrub, producing bushy growth and attractive rich green leaves. If not deadheaded, it produces orange-red rosehips, which can look particularly attractive into winter. Knock Out responds well to rich soil conditions and benefits from regular feeding, which helps to continue its long flowering display.

Floribunda | 2000
H: 1m x S: 1m

TRUMPETER
(see page 71)

This is a really popular Floribunda and deserves its good reputation. It has compact growth and produces brilliant scarlet semi-double to double flowers from early summer through to late autumn, growing in clusters of between three and fifteen. The plant always looks as if it's completely covered in flowers. Trumpeter is happiest grown in a sunny spot with free-draining soil. It responds well to feeding, especially after its first flush of flowers, and only requires light pruning.

Floribunda | 1977
H: 60cm x S: 50cm

FRAGRANT CLOUD
(see page 14)

This must truly rate as one of the most sweetly scented roses I know. It's a strong-growing, healthy rose which will flower continuously throughout the summer. I have seen descriptions of it being geranium-red, coral and even orange but, for me, it's more a vermilion-red shade. The flowers open from beautifully shaped buds and, though it is a Hybrid Tea, they often appear in clusters of between three and five. The flowers are double and well-formed and hold their colour, not fading like many red roses. It can be prone to mildew and if the weather is very damp early on, there can be trouble with blackspot. However, with good cultivation, these problems can be controlled. It makes an excellent cut flower and I enjoy bringing the flowers indoors where you can get close to the penetrating scent. In warmer countries, it can be grown as a climber where it will easily reach 1.8–2 metres.

Hybrid Tea | 1967
H: 1.5m x S: 1m

INGRID BERGMAN
(see page 101)

Ingrid Bergman is one of my favourite roses to use as a cut flower and is one of the best red Hybrid Tea roses you can grow. It carries perfectly shaped buds and flowers of a magnificent rich red. It makes a strong, bushy plant with excellent foliage. There are very few, if any, problems with disease. It has a light rose scent and continues flowering from June until the first frosts.

Hybrid Tea | 1984
H: 80cm x S: 70cm

INTRIGUE
(see page 23)

This rose only has a light scent but it makes up for this by producing stunning blooms of the darkest red in clusters of up to twenty. The flowers are small, double and open from buds that are nearly black to rich, deep, velvety red blooms. The plant is vigorous but low-growing and its floral display lasts through the season. It stands up well to rain and heat. The only problem I have found is that the foliage it can be prone to blackspot. It makes a gorgeous cut flower.

Floribunda | 1978
H: 75cm x S: 75cm

LE ROUGE ET LE NOIR

This is a French Hybrid Tea – a magnificent red with an exceptionally good scent – raised by the famous breeder Delbard. The flowers are large and double and the colour is a deep, velvety red, with the edge of the petals darker, giving a rich effect overall to each blossom. The scent, with its hints of vanilla and citrus, matches this richness. The foliage is dark green and glossy with good disease-resistance. The flowers are produced on long stems, making them ideal for cutting. It's not excessively thorny and is an excellent rose for growing in borders.

Hybrid Tea | 1973
H: 1m x S: 1m

MARIAN FINUCANE
(see page 72)

A charming new Irish rose, 'Marian Finucane' is a Floribunda with attractive small double flowers of an unusual bronze-red colour. It has a delicious fragrance which is sweet and light close up. The growth is bushy and compact and the foliage is mid-green and has good disease-resistance. An excellent rose for containers, it also makes a very attractive cut flower. 'Marian Finucane' should only be lightly pruned to keep its overall shape tidy. It benefits from being mulched and really appreciates good feeding. Position it in a bright, sunny spot in free-draining soil.

Floribunda | 2005
H: 60cm x S: 80cm

PAPA MEILLAND
(see page 15)

To get the best from this rose, it needs a warm climate. The moist, humid conditions I have in Ireland encourage mildew. I've tried it and I'm afraid, though it grows and flowers, it's never as good as it can be. But if you're lucky enough to live in warmer, drier climes, you should have better luck. It is slow to establish and dislikes cold and frost in winter. Ideally, you need a warm, sunny, sheltered spot with good drainage. A tall, upright-growing rose with prickly stems, it never seems to be covered in flowers but makes up for this with its quality of colour and scent. There is also a climbing version, released in 1970.

Hybrid Tea | 1970
H: 1.2m x S: 2m

RUBY WEDDING
(see page 127)

'Ruby Wedding' is an attractive Hybrid Tea. The flowers are crimson-red and the foliage is a particularly good dark glossy green. It makes a very bushy plant and has a long flowering period. The scent is light and sweet. This rose grows well in containers or can be positioned towards the front of a border.

Hybrid Tea | 1979
H: 1.25m x S: 80cm

purple-red

BIG PURPLE

This is truly a sumptuous rose raised in New Zealand. The flowers are large and beautifully shaped with a sweet, very strong fragrance. They are  produced on single stems and are a flower arranger's dream, especially as they're a rather special purple-crimson colour. Unfortunately, the flowers don't tolerate rain very well, so it's a rose that's better suited to drier climates. The foliage is healthy, the growth is upright, and it's a reliable repeat-flowerer. This rose should be planted in a sunny, sheltered position, where it is protected from wind.

Hybrid Tea | 1985
H: 1.75m x S: 1m

purple-violet

MAMMY BLUE
(see page 102)

This exquisite rose by Delbard produces attractive Hybrid Tea-shaped flowers of a gorgeous and unusual lilac colour. It makes a tidy, bushy plant and the flowers are superb for cutting. Flower arrangers will love it. It responds well to good soil and a sunny position.

Hybrid Tea
H: 1m x S: 1m

YESTERDAY

This pretty rose has single pink flowers, flushed purple-crimson with a white centre and a tidy tuft of golden stamens. The flowers fade to an attractive pink and are borne in large clusters of up to twenty-five. It's a rose that repeat-flowers very well, continuing far into autumn. It is excellent for a mixed planting and combines superbly with herbaceous perennials. To get the best from this rose, plant it in a sunny spot in good-quality, free-draining soil. An annual mulch will make all the difference to the quality of its blooms.

Floribunda | 1974
H: 1m x S: 1m

soft pink

BLESSINGS
(see page 126)

If you're looking for a Floribunda rose with exceptionally good colour, this is one to choose. The flowers open from shapely buds to produce full double flowers of a combination of rich to soft coral-pink. The foliage is healthy and dark green and has very good disease-resistance. It produces an exceptional quantity of flower, which makes this rose outstanding. It's ideal for cutting and withstands rainy weather extremely well.

Floribunda | 1967
H: 80cm x S: 60cm

DAINTY BESS
(see page 92)

This single Hybrid Tea repeat-flowers exceptionally well and the flowers are a delicate soft pink. The central boss of stamens is clearly visible. The foliage is dark green and the stems are quite thorny. It can be prone to blackspot. This rose should be grown in a sheltered, sunny spot. It appreciates good, well-drained soil and will benefit from the application of an annual mulch.

Hybrid Tea | 1925
H: 1m x S: 1m

DIORESSENCE
(see page 105)

I can highly recommend this rose for its exceptional fragrance and exquisite pink and lilac colouring. Since its introduction, it has received popular acclaim for these special qualities. Its foliage is healthy and it enjoys a sunny, sheltered spot.

Hybrid Tea | 1984
H: 1m x S: 1m

SAVOY HOTEL

This rose sports large, perfectly shaped Hybrid Tea flowers of the most beautiful silver-pink with deeper-coloured centres that unfold in a gorgeous swirl. It's bushy with good vigour and healthy growth and it has a medium to sweet scent. It looks splendid planted in a group and also makes an excellent bedding rose, as well as a good cut flower since it lasts well in water. A large bunch of this rose is a magnificent sight. Always eye-catching and  never overpowering, it's an exceptional plant which should be grown for its colour and beautifully shaped flowers.

Hybrid Tea | 1987
H: 1m x S: 75cm

ANNA LIVIA
(see page 108)

'Anna Livia' was presented to the City of Dublin to mark its millennium in 1988. It produces attractively-shaped salmon-pink, semi-double flowers that are paler towards the centre. The flower petals can be marked by rain. Flowers are produced in clusters of between five and fifteen on long stems, which makes them perfect for cutting. It's a strong, healthy rose, attractive when planted in groups.

Floribunda | 1985
H: 1.75m x S: 1.25m

CONGRATULATIONS
(see page 127)

Contratulations makes a very attractive, tall-growing Floribunda rose that produces silvery pink flowers. It's a typical Floribunda except that the flowers open from Hybrid Tea-shaped buds. It has good disease-resistance and it makes an excellent cut flower. The fragrance is medium to sweet. Because of its height it makes a superb hedging rose.

Floribunda | 1979
H: 2m x S: 1.25m

SEXY REXY
(see page 73)

This was introduced from New Zealand in 1984 by the famous rose breeders, McGredy's. It is a Floribunda that produces a plentiful display of small, perfectly formed pink flowers and it has a tidy habit. The flowers are darker in the centre and pale towards the edges. Once established, the clusters can carry as many as fifteen flowers. I recommend deadheading to encourage continuous

blooming. This is a rose with good disease-resistance. It's also extremely long-lasting as a cut flower. Sexy Rexy responds well to being grown in an open, sunny spot. Light pruning is required as well as free-draining soil.

Floribunda | 1984
H: 75cm x S: 60cm

VALENTINE HEART

The semi-double flowers of Valentine Heart are an attractive two-tone pink, dark on the outside and pale within. Bred by Dixon of Northern Ireland, this rose is very tolerant of wet weather conditions. The flowers appear in clusters of five to fifteen  and are held on long stems which, along with its ability to last a long time in water, means it is super as a cut flower. Its scent is sweet and strong. It flowers continuously but should be deadheaded to guarantee this.

Floribunda | 1989
H: 1.25 x S: 75cm

WARM WISHES
(see page 125)

This rose has won many awards and is a strong-growing Hybrid Tea of great character. The flower shape and colour have great charm. The colour is a mixture of pink and apricot with dark tones towards the centre. In hot climates, the flower gradually fades to pink and soft cream. Each flower is large and the petals curl back. It produces dark green, healthy foliage and repeat-flowers very well. The scent is medium to fruity.

Hybrid Tea | 1994
H: 1m x S: 75cm

CENTENAIRE DE LOURDES
(see page 119)

This good French Floribunda from the late 1950s usually starts to flower late in the summer, but it continues well into autumn. The scent is medium and sweet and the foliage is good. It makes an excellent cut flower. It is also noted for its magnificent display of orange-coloured rosehips which carry the interest on into winter.

Floribunda | 1958
H: 1.5m x S: 1.75m

NOSTALGIA

This great Hybrid Tea was raised in Germany. Its large flowers have a central swirl of ivory-white petals, while the outer petals turn a rich crimson to cherry-red at the very edges. It opens its flowers slowly, which adds to the longevity of the blooms. It has a powerful sweet scent and makes a bushy, compact, tidy plant that never gets too tall. The foliage is healthy. You can expect a good display of flowers right through the season. It makes  an excellent cut flower, as it not only looks good in flower arrangements, but also has the ability to hold well in water.

Hybrid Tea | 1996
H: 1m x S: 80cm

shrub roses

DAMASK, ENGLISH ROSES, GALLICA, GROUND COVER ROSES, HYBRID MUSK, MODERN SHRUB ROSES, RUGOSA

Shrub roses generally make large, bushy plants. They usually require less pruning than Hybrid Tea and Floribunda roses and are extremely valuable as specimen plants. Many provide the added bonus of having hips which can be appreciated through the winter months.

white-cream

BLANCHE DOUBLE DE COUBERT
(see page 80)

Probably the most popular Rugosa rose, 'Blanche Double de Coubert' produces exquisite double, white, scented flowers. The foliage is bright green and has a crinkled texture. It is extremely disease-resistant and is an excellent choice for growing in coastal areas. Give this rose a sunny spot. When it's established, it's tolerant of exposed positions. It requires very little pruning and appreciates occasional feeding to help encourage good flowering.

Rugosa Hybrid | 1892
H: 1.5m x S: 1.5m

JACQUELINE DU PRÉ
(see page 68)

Jacqueline du Pré is a very beautiful rose. Its colour is cream, with the palest pink tinge on the reverse of the petals. The filaments in the centre of the flower are exposed. They are long and darker pink in colour, creating an attractive contrast to the petals. It's quite a thorny rose with a light scent.

Feeding after the rose's first flush of flowers encourages a continuous display. Jacqueline du Pré has excellent disease-resistance and will happily grow in sun or light shade.

Shrub Rose | 1988
H: 1.75m x S: 1.25m

KENT
(see page 84)

This is an outstanding ground cover rose, producing clusters of small semi-double to double white flowers. It has a light, soft, musky scent and the dark, glossy green foliage is extremely healthy. The plant is vigorous and has really good disease-resistance. It flowers throughout the season until first frosts and is particularly good when grown to cover a bank or large area. Be careful not to over-prune this rose; a little goes a long way. It's happy when grown in a sheltered, sunny spot and it responds well to mulching and feeding.

Ground Cover | 1988
H: 75cm x S: 1.25m

LITTLE WHITE PET
(see page 69)

Sometimes just called 'White Pet', this is a super, low-growing, spreading rose that is ideally suited to growing in containers. It repeat-flowers well and produces white pompon-like button flowers in big trusses throughout the summer. Its foliage is healthy and a clear green colour, which sets off its flowers beautifully. The scent is good with a hint of musk. This rose needs to be deadheaded, as it tends to hold onto its flowers after they have turned brown. 'Little White Pet' is happiest when grown in a sunny position. It is generally disease-resistant.

Sempervirens Hybrid | 1879
H: 60cm x S: 60cm

MADAME HARDY
(see page 110)

This rose is exceptional in every way. The scent is delicate, yet opulent, with undertones of citrus and lemon. The blooms are fully double and the petals surround a central green eye. The outermost petals are reflexed and the central petals are ruffled and quartered. The flowers appear in clusters of three to five. Sadly, they may be damaged by rain. It makes a vigorous bush and the foliage tends to be generally healthy, only occasionally getting a touch of blackspot.

Damask Rose | 1832
H: 2m x S: 1.5m

NEVADA
(see page 32)

'Nevada' is an attractive shrub rose with arching growth and good height, making it ideal for hedging. Its stems are covered in ivory-white, single to semi-double flowers which gradually turn pure white as the flowers age. Its main flush is in June and it produces an intermittent display of flowers late in the season. The foliage is an attractive mid-green. It has to be one of the easiest shrub roses to grow, as it makes very few demands, even though it takes a few years to establish. Ultimately, it's a strong-growing plant with good foliage and very few, if any, thorns. I have grown this rose on a north-facing wall and have found it to be happy in shade, but it will perform equally well in sun. Pruning is really just done to tidy the plant.

Shrub Rose | 1927
H: 3m x S: 4m

PENELOPE
(see page 116)

One of the most popular Hybrid Musk roses, producing plentiful clusters of palest shell-pink fragrant flowers, which quickly turn white as they mature. The scent is sweet and musky. Its growth is spreading and gently arching. If you deadhead, you are guaranteed late blooms, but if not you can expect a good winter display of hips. A healthy plant with good disease-resistant foliage.

Hybrid Musk | 1924
H: 2m x S: 2m

SALLY HOLMES

This is a really showy rose, producing enormous clusters of Floribunda-like

flowers with single, floppy petals of ivory-white. The flowers open cream, flushed pink, and fade to white. The stems are strong and can carry up to forty flowers. It repeat-flowers very well and the scent is light and musky. The foliage is mid-green. It is generally disease-resistant but can occasionally get hit by blackspot. The flowers may be marked by wet weather or damaged by wind, so this rose is best positioned in a sheltered spot.

Shrub Rose | 1976
H: 1.5m x S: 2m

R. SERICEA SUBSP. OMEIENSIS F. PTERACANTHA
(see page 38)

This is a truly remarkable Species rose. It's grown for its unusual thorny growth, which can be very eye-catching. Old growth will require regular pruning, as this encourages new stems which carry the brightest-coloured thorns. If you're looking for a rose to intimidate a prospective burglar, this is the one to have. It doesn't suffer from disease and is happy when grown in full sun in free-draining soil. It appreciates an annual mulch of well-rotted organic matter. The foliage is bright green, small and fern-like.

Species | 1890
H: 3m x S: 2m

AGNES
(see page 81)

This is a glorious, yellow-flowered Rugosa hybrid. It flowers once early in the season and has an unusual light and fruity scent. It originated in Canada and is a superb garden rose. It's not the best in wet weather conditions but it does produce its flowers over a long period, which makes up for this. It can be prone to blackspot and rust, so plant in an open position with plenty of sunshine and provide good soil. Light pruning is required. It is not a fussy rose and, once established, it is not very demanding, but it does appreciate occasional feeding.

Rugosa hybrid | 1900
H: 2m x S: 2.5m

CHARLOTTE

Charlotte is very closely related to the rose Graham Thomas (see page 138) – it also produces globular flowers. They are a rich yellow and the shape is flat on top. The colour eventually fades to a creamy lemon-yellow. They appear in clusters of up to five. The foliage is pale green and large, and the growth is

upright and bushy. This rose is best lightly pruned during the dormant period, which will encourage a good shape. It may need treatment for blackspot and mildew.

Shrub Rose | 1993
H: 1m x S: 75cm

FRÜHLINGSGOLD
(see page 34)

This showy rose is often used for public-area plantings. The buds are pointed, with streaks of orange, and they open into large primrose-yellow flowers with cream to yellow tones, with the colour deepening towards the centre. As it has a single to semi-double flower, you can appreciate the dark stamens in the centre, which help to intensify the yellow, making it look buttery. The flowers are carried in clusters and sometimes singly along the stem. They appear on last year's stems, which are usually arching, and the effect is very pleasing when this rose is in full flower. It has excellent disease-resistance and should be grown in an open, sunny position where there is no competition from other plants, such as overhanging trees. Light pruning is recommended.

Spinosissima Hybrid | 1937
H: 2.5m x S: 3m

GRAHAM THOMAS
(see page 104)

This has to be one of the most widely grown of all of David Austin's roses. Its rich, golden-yellow colour is uncommonly good and the plant is extremely free-flowering. The flower scent is a fresh Tea Rose fragrance. It can be grown as a bush or a freestanding shrub. Its foliage is healthy and provides an exceptionally good foil to its full flowers.

Shrub Rose | 1983
H: 1.75m (3m as a climber) x S: 1.75m

SAINT ALBAN

This rose carries cup-shaped lemon-yellow flowers of great charm. The flowers hang their heads slightly and have a delicious, fresh scent which is difficult to describe. Saint Alban makes a medium-sized bush, with its stems arching gracefully and with a lax character. The light green foliage is disease-resistant. Not the best rose for wet conditions, as flowers may fail to fully develop, so plant it in a warm, sheltered spot in your garden. It really appreciates the protection of other plants such as a hedge, which will shelter it from rain.

Shrub Rose | 2003
H: 1.2m x S: 1m

THE PILGRIM

I'm very fond of this rose. It's exceptionally prolific in its production of flowers, with clusters of up to fifteen on a stem. The flowers are large and flat-topped and are yellow, turning to lemon and then fading to cream. The petals are quilled and tightly packed, creating a neat effect.

It's a strong, vigorous grower with very few thorns. It's important to deadhead if you want it to re-bloom. The fragrance is a delicious mixture of fruit and musk. This rose should be pruned lightly, a job best done in the dormant season.

Shrub Rose | 1991
H: 1.5m x S: 1.25m

R. XANTHINA 'CANARY BIRD'
(syn. 'Canary Bird')

I came across 'Canary Bird' in my first job working in a nursery. There it was grown and sold as a standard, producing a lovely weeping effect. It's in full flower from April into early May. The blooms are single and bright yellow and are very eye-catching – like jewels against the green foliage. Sadly, the flowering period is brief, although there are sometimes more flowers in autumn. The growth is strong. It looks especially well when underplanted with late spring-flowering bulbs.

Xanthina Hybrid | 1911
H: 2.5m x S: 4m

GOLDEN CELEBRATION
(see page 124)

This is a stunning yellow rose, the centre of which is a rich egg-yolk yellow. It is also noted for its wonderful strong scent. The stems have very few thorns and the foliage is glossy and mid-green. It occasionally succumbs to blackspot but is generally a healthy rose. It looks great when planted in groups and could even be used as a short climber against a low wall, where its hanging flowers can really be appreciated.

Shrub Rose | 1992
H: 1.25m x S: 1m

GRACE

A lovely rose with attractive arching stems, Grace combines beautifully with Golden Celebration (see left). The flowers are perfectly formed and are reproduced in long bunches. The colour is a mixture of shades of apricot and orange. The fragrance is rich and warm, sweet and sensuous, and the growth is vigorous and healthy. Grace forms a medium-sized shrub and repeat-flowers well throughout the summer. It is great for planting in blocks, where its colour impact will be seen from a distance. It benefits from an annual mulch and regular feeding.

Shrub Rose | 2001
H: 1.25m x S: 1m

PERLE D'OR

The flowers on this rose are small and perfectly formed, giving it great charm and elegance. The deep pink buds open to a rich apricot-pink, gradually fading to shell-pink on the outside as the flower develops. The flowers can be sparse, but if you nurture it with rich growing conditions, you'll be

rewarded with quite large sprays of flowers. Thorns are few but large and the leaves are healthy and dark green. It will flower continually in a warm spot and needs little, if any, pruning.

Polyantha | 1883
H: 1m x S: 1m

peach, buff & copper

ABRAHAM DARBY
(see page 94)

Large, fully double, cup-shaped flowers with a glorious scent grace this rose. The colour is apricot, orange, yellow and peach combined with pink. I am particularly fond of the ripe-fruit fragrance. Foliage is rich green and glossy, though it can be susceptible to blackspot. Good growing conditions are needed to get the best from this stunning rose. An open, sunny position is preferable. Do not prune too hard, as this will impair flowering. It's also important to deadhead this rose to ensure repeat flowering it benefits from regular feeding and a mulch, especially in hot summers.

English Rose | 1985
H: 1.5m x S: 1.25m

ARCHIDUC JOSEPH

This is a super rose for growing in a mixed border because of its compact size, and it can be positioned towards the front, thanks to its lack of thorns. Its dominant colour is pink but there is shading of orange, peach and sometimes subtle purple

tones, too. The colour varies depending on the positioning and amount of sunlight. It has a delicate but long-lasting perfume and, for an old rose, it has remarkable strength and vigour. It responds to good-quality soil, which will ensure you get the best from its flowers.

Tea Rose | 1872
H: 1.5m x W: 1m

CORNELIA
(see page 66)

'Cornelia' is a Hybrid Musk of great beauty. It produces clusters of soft apricot-pink flowers which fade gradually to a creamy pink, all starting from coral-coloured buds. The scent is excellent, sweet and musky. The foliage is light green and the plant is very vigorous. It's especially good for growing over arches or pergolas. To get the best from this rose, provide good-quality garden soil. It benefits from regular feeding and appreciates a mulch to keep in moisture during the summer months. It has generally good disease-resistance and pruning is only recommended for keeping the plant tidy and in shape.

Hybrid Musk | 1925
H: 1.5m (4m when trained as climber) x S: 1.75m

CROWN PRINCESS MARGARETA
(see page 111)

One of David Austin's most striking apricot-orange coloured roses, Crown Princess Margareta produces a rounded bush, the stems being slightly arching in their growth. The medium-sized flowers are shallow and cup-shaped. When fully open, they become a lovely soft apricot colour. They have a fruity fragrance with undertones of tea. The foliage is plentiful and glossy. This rose can also be grown against a wall as a climber.

Shrub Rose | 1999
H: 1.75m x S: 1.5m

EVELYN

The unique scent of this David Austin rose is a mixture of sugar, freshly sliced apricots and peaches. You could almost eat it. The flowers are large and an amazing colour – peachy pink with apricot and honey tones  towards the centre, paler towards the edges. As the bloom expands and ages, the overall effect is of gentle fading. It has a button eye and a cupped shape but the shape changes as it progresses to a fully blown bloom. The foliage is pale green but, I'm sad to say that, in my experience, it's very prone to blackspot. I've been tempted to stop growing it, but it's difficult because I'm addicted to the delicious fragrance.

Shrub Rose | 1991
H: 1.25m x S: 1.25m

PEGASUS

If, like me, you love the Hybrid Musk rose 'Buff Beauty' (see page 157), you'll love Pegasus, too. This David Austin rose produces beautiful, large, full flowers of a soft apricot-buff colour that pales at the edges to cream. They are borne as single flowers or in small  clusters and are long-lasting, making them ideal as cut flowers. The fragrance is strong – a combination of tea and ripe

fruit – and the foliage has good disease-resistance. Growth is arching and the stems have very few thorns.

Shrub Rose | 1995
H: 1.25m x S: 1m

SWEET JULIET

An unusually coloured rose with flowers in a mixture of peach, apricot, pink and buff, its petals are darker on the reverse, while the outer petals are quite pale. Flowers are produced singly or in clusters. It really enjoys a warm climate where it repeat-flowers well. The fragrance is strong and fruity. This rose looks best when planted in groups of either three or five or  can be trained as an attractive pillar rose. Make sure the soil is well drained and that Sweet Juliet is positioned in the sun.

Shrub Rose | 1989
H: 1.2m x S: 90cm

TEASING GEORGIA

The flowers of this rose have a rich scent that's best described as strong, sweet and fruity. The colour is sumptuous – creamy-white edged with gold and yellow, with shades of buff, honey and lemon in between, adding great character and depth to the cup-shaped, quartered flowers. The flowers are inclined to hang because of their weight. The growth is lax and pruning is needed to keep the plant compact. In warm gardens,

Teasing Georgia can be grown as a low climber, or it can be grown on supports, such as pergolas or freestanding pillars.

Shrub Rose | 1998
H: 1.5m x S: 1m

THE ALEXANDRA ROSE

Not what you usually expect from a David Austin rose. Stunning, single flowers of a light, fresh salmon-pink unfold from copper-tinged buds, fading almost to white before the petals fall. The clusters can consist of as many as twenty on a stem. It produces very few thorns and is generally a healthy plant that repeat-flowers well, giving a super show right into autumn. The Alexandra Rose favours a sunny,  sheltered spot and responds to regular feeding and mulching. It is great for mixed borders, as it associates well with other plants.

Shrub Rose | 1994
H: 1.5m x S: 1.25m

HENRI MARTIN
(see page 75)

This is an exquisite Moss rose with exceptionally beautiful flowers, which start a crimson-red and eventually mature with purple tones. It is strong-growing and has very good disease-resistance. The stems are extremely thorny. It is easy to grow in most gardens and tolerates poor soil conditions. 'Henri Martin' does not require hard pruning. It must have a free-draining soil, but it would also benefit from the application of a mulch for the summer months.

Moss Rose | 1863
H: 1.5m x S: 1.25m

MRS ANTHONY WATERER
(see page 82)

If you're looking for a foolproof rose, it's hard to beat many of the Rugosa hybrids, including this one. They really are sturdy, requiring very little pruning, not suffering from disease, and ideal for situations in coastal gardens, as they will tolerate salt spray. The red flowers on 'Mrs Anthony Waterer' are beautiful. I'm very fond of the lavender tinge which appears. This rose also has an exceptionally good fragrance, which is really sweet. The foliage is remarkable too, being rich green with a lovely corrugated texture. It makes a good hedging rose or it can be used as a specimen plant. It's particularly thorny, so be careful when pruning, which is not often needed.

Rugosa Hybrid | 1898
H: 1.5m x S: 2m

PRINCE CAMILLE DE ROHAN

This antique rose is a combination of different shades of red – dark maroon, rich red, deepest crimson and a touch of black. The scent is medium to sweet and the flowers, which appear in small clusters or singly, are inclined to nod and hang their heads. It's best planted in a bright spot out of direct sunlight, which can scorch the petals, and it needs good-quality soil. With this rose, the secret of success lies in feeding, disease-prevention and correct watering. Though it's not the strongest and showiest of roses,

'Prince Camille de Rohan' has great character and is worthy of special attention. A sport of this beautiful rose is 'Roger Lambelin', the petals of which are flecked and flashed with white.

Hybrid Perpetual | 1861
H: 1.25m x S: 1

crimson & deep red

EMPEREUR DU MAROC
(see page 21)

Of all the dark red roses I grow, this is the one that's nearest to black. Its rich, heady fragrance is a match for the colour and its petals have a lovely velvet sheen. As with many of these deep red roses, I have found that it is not the strongest grower, but that could just be under Irish gardening conditions. I find it needs extra care and attention if you are to get the best from it. I classify 'Empereur du Maroc' as one of my greedy roses; it really responds well to extra feeding and special care. I grow it in a bright spot but out of direct sunlight as this can scorch the flowers and turn the outer petals brown.

Hybrid Perpetual | 1858
H: 1.5m x S: 1.25m

FALSTAFF

This is a fabulous crimson rose – one of the best for colour – from David

Austin's stable. The large flowers are shallow-cupped and packed full of petals. The deep crimson colour gradually fades towards the outer petals and, as the rose ages, it changes to a shade of magenta-

crimson. The foliage is large and looks more like that of a modern rose than of an old rose. It is prone to blackspot. The scent is strong, sweet and old-fashioned. Falstaff repeat-flowers well, but only if deadheaded. Grown as a climber, it can be trained to around three metres.

Shrub Rose | 1999
H: 1.5m x S: 1.5m

L. D. BRAITHWAITE
(see page 24)

This is one of David Austin's finest. Its light-crimson flowers are an exceptionally good colour and are produced in clusters of up to five per stem. Each flower is cupped, and the loosely filled centre is surrounded by broad, reflexed petals, creating a beautiful and attractive shape. It also repeats well, producing blooms continuously throughout the flowering season. The flowers need to mature on the plant before releasing an old-rose fragrance. For best results, L.D. Braithwaite should be grown in a bright, sunny position. It really benefits from the application of a mulch, which helps to keep in valuable moisture during the warm days of summer. The foliage is a rich, green colour and can be a little prone to blackspot. However, with good management, this should never become a serious problem.

Shrub Rose | 1988
H: 1m x S: 1m

LOUIS XIV

I have included this rose, despite the fact that its growth is spindly and light. It's here because of its magnificent colouring and scent. The flowers are the darkest crimson-red – deeper than almost any other rose I know bar 'Sénégal' (see page 159). The scent is intoxicating, heavy and rich.This rose

needs extra care – plenty of good feeding, watering and a sheltered spot. It's happy in hot climates. Sadly, it's also susceptible to blackspot and mildew. So you might say, 'Why grow it?' When you've seen it and smelled its flowers, you'll understand why. It remains a rose for the collector.

China Rose | 1859
H: 60cm x S: 60cm

TESS OF THE D'URBERVILLES

This is a gorgeous, dark crimson rose. The flowers open from almost black buds and have a light, sweet scent. They are large and heavy and can hang. It can be grown as a low climber, where the hanging flowers

become an asset. The stems are very thorny and, when grown well, can produce clusters of up to four flowers per stem. This is one of my favourite David Austin roses. It should be lightly pruned in winter and will grow in sun or shade.

Shrub Rose | 1998
H: 1.7m x S: 1.25m

THE DARK LADY

The name of this rose is deceptive, as the flowers are a bright crimson colour and the backs of the petals are pale. The flower is loose and very attractive and has a strong, sweet scent. Flowers appear singly or in clusters of up to three and the stems are very thorny. It's not a particularly vigorous grower but has an attractive, spreading habit. You need to keep an eye out for mildew and it's important to deadhead. The Dark Lady is a rose that looks great when planted in blocks of three or five for most impact.

Shrub Rose | 1991
H: 80cm x S: 1m

TUSCANY SUPERB

The flowers on 'Tuscany Superb' are larger than those of 'Tuscany' and are a fabulous deep-purple shade, which is exaggerated by the bright yellow stamens. I'm particularly fond of the velvet texture and look

of its petals. The flowers are produced singly or in small clusters of up to three. It has very few thorns and the fragrance is light and sweet. It needs good cultivation and really benefits from having the soil prepared in advance of planting. An annual mulch and regular feeding will make all the difference when it comes to the quality of flowers.

Gallica | 1837
H: 1.5m x S: 1.25m

WILLIAM SHAKESPEARE 2000
(see page 25)

The flowers of this disease-resistant rose by David Austin are truly stunning. This is a very special red rose which can also be used as a cut flower, as it lasts well in water, and you can really get close to the blooms to appreciate their superb colour and velvety texture. I have found that this rose really responds well to a deep mulching. This keeps its roots cool and moist in summer, which it seems to enjoy. It's also important to prune it well, removing all of its weak growth. The best position is in an open, sunny spot, sheltered from wind. Foliage is bright to mid-green.

Shrub Rose | 2000
H: 1.5m x S: 1.25m

purple-red

CARDINAL DE RICHELIEU
(see page 42)

A rose with a remarkable purple colour. The flowers are an attractive shape and are fully double. They are small and usually come in clusters of two or three and are scented, but not excessively so. The dark green foliage is small and the stems are generally thornless. I have seen this rose grown as a hedge but for this you will need good-quality garden soil. A warm position is best, especially in more northerly gardens. It must be grown in free-draining soil, especially when establishing. It can be prone to disease and in some years may be attacked by mildew. Mulching and regular feeding keep this rose in good condition. Pruning should not be too heavy.

Gallica | 1845
H: 1.75m x S: 1.5m

CHARLES DE MILLS
(see page 35)

The blooms of 'Charles de Mills' are exquisitely shaped and, when fully open, you can appreciate their stunning colours. The scent is light. It's a vigorous, bushy plant that can be used both as a specimen and as an informal hedge. It's best grown in a sunny position in well-drained soil. The foliage is healthy and generally free from disease. Avoid hard pruning; pruning should really concentrate on keeping a good bushy shape to the plant.

Gallica | 1790
H: 1.5m x S: 1.75m

ROSERAIE DE L'HAŸ
(see page 83)

If you're looking for a trouble-free tough rose with healthy foliage, you can't go far wrong with 'Roseraie de l'Haÿ'. The flower is magenta-pink and richly fragrant. It makes an attractive specimen plant or a useful hedge. It's particularly good as a rose for coastal areas, where it can tolerate a salt-laden breeze, and is happy to grow in poor soil. 'Roseraie de l'Haÿ' is happiest when grown in an open, sunny spot. The foliage is bright green and corrugated. The soil should be well-drained and, to encourage a good floral display, it's a good idea to feed and mulch this rose annually. It requires little pruning, but you will need to wear gloves when doing this, as it's a very thorny rose.

Rugosa hybrid | 1901
H: 1.75m x S: 2m

WILLIAM LOBB

This is probably the most glorious

purple Moss rose I know. It's extremely strong-growing and produces long, thorny stems. The flowers grow in mossed clusters and start a magenta-purple, then take on mauve, lavender and lilac tones, ending with a grey wash. It is occasionally susceptible to blackspot and attack from mildew. I have grown this in several gardens and I've tried it in both sunny and shady spots, where it has performed exceptionally well. I have also used it as an informal hedge. It benefits from an annual mulch of well-rotted organic matter.

Moss Rose | 1855
H: 2.5m x S: 1.5m

---

purple-violet

BELLE DE CRÉCY
(see page 91)

This rose is noted for its exceptional flower colour, which embraces varying shades of magenta, lilac and pink. The flowers are fully double and quartered in the centre as they open. The foliage is dark green and the stems are very thorny. Occasionally, mildew is a problem but this can easily be dealt with by using proprietary fungal treatments. The plant benefits from good cultivation. An open, sunny position, mulching and regular feeding all make a difference to the quality of this plant and its blooms.

Gallica | 1829
H: 1m x S: 1m

REINE DES VIOLETTES
(see page 44)

This has to be one of the most uniquely and exquisitely coloured of all the old-fashioned roses. The medium-sized flowers, which are fully double and flat in shape, open a deep pink and then fade to shades of gentle lilac with tones of grey. The stems are smooth and thornless and the foliage is matt and dull green. It repeat-flowers very well and has a lovely old-world rose fragrance. It makes a compact plant and really benefits from being planted in a warm, sunny, sheltered spot. Good feeding and mulching make a difference to the quality of the flowers. It can be prone to disease and it's important to keep an eye out for blackspot, and mildew in some seasons.

Hybrid Perpetual | 1860
H: 2m x S: 1.5m

RHAPSODY IN BLUE
(see page 19)

The first thing to note about this award-winning rose is its exceptional colour – not true blue but a combination of mauve and slate blue that appears iridescent purple in some lights. It has also won awards for its sweet, penetrating fragrance. The growth is tall and bushy and it repeat-flowers extremely well. The foliage is rich green and healthy. To encourage continuous flowering, you need to deadhead. Also, the positioning of this rose makes a difference. A pale background will highlight its unusually coloured flowers. Popular with flower arrangers, thanks to its unusual colour, it also makes an exquisite border plant if cleverly combined with herbaceous perennials.

Shrub Rose | 1999
H: 1.5m x S: 1m

blush

A SHROPSHIRE LAD
(see page 62)

Introduced in 1996, this David Austin rose produces cup-shaped peachy pink flowers of exceptional quality, with a fruity, delicious scent. It is one of the best roses for growing on arches and pergolas. Do not prune this rose too hard and, if growing it as a climber, it will be necessary to tie it into the support. It produces a great display of large flowers. Foliage is healthy and generally disease-resistant. It's important to deadhead and feed regularly through the summer. Not to be confused with another rose called 'Shropshire Lass'.

Shrub Rose | 1996
H: 2m x S: 1.25m

BELLE ISIS

This is a charming and very beautiful pale pink Gallica. As with other

Gallicas, the flowers are quartered around a small central green eye. They grow abundantly, either singly or in clusters of up to five or six and are held well above the healthy, pale green foliage. The scent is a combination of myrrh and musk with bitter overtones. 'Belle Isis' is once-flowering and its stems are sometimes weighed down by the fullness and weight of its flowers. A few bamboo canes carefully positioned just before the flowers open can give this beauty the extra support it needs.

Gallica | 1845
H: 1.75m x S: 1.25m

NOZOMI
(see page 87)

This has become a classic ground cover rose, raised in Japan where it's often used in rock gardens. The stems form an interesting zigzag pattern as they grow. The pale shell-pink flowers are small and delicate. The petals don't overlap and, at first glance, they are like large apple blossoms. The leaves are tiny, dark green and healthy. The scent of the flowers is light and musky. This small-growing rose really only needs the minimum of pruning. It will grow in sun or light shade and responds best to free-draining soil. Some occasional feeding will encourage a good flowering display.

Ground Cover | 1968
H: 50cm x S: 1.5m

SHARIFA ASMA

This is one of David Austin's most beautiful and sweetly scented roses, with strong fruity notes of mulberry and white grape, and a touch of myrrh, musk and sugar. The flower is a soft pink, starting from bud with a quartered centre, and opening to a loosely-filled,

cup-shaped flower full of petals. The disease-resistance is good, though it is susceptible to blackspot. For a good display of flowers, it needs rich soil and plenty of water in the growing season. It makes a fantastic cut flower. I have seen this stunning rose grown en masse, where it always creates a dramatic impact.

Shrub Rose | 1989
H: 1.25m x S: 1m

SOUVENIR DE SAINT ANNE'S

This is a superb single-flowering sport of 'Souvenir de la Malmaison' that has become popular in rose collections throughout the world. It was saved from extinction when it was given by Lady Moore to Graham Stuart Thomas in the 1950s. Its petals are a delicate, soft pink fading to white and it is continuously in flower, often producing flowers right up to Christmas Day in my own garden. It's a real treasure and benefits from good feeding and an annual mulch. I prune lightly after Christmas, removing buds and seedheads, which I believe gives the rose a rest before it starts again in the new season.

Bourbon | 1950
H: 1.5m x S: 1m

THE SHEPHERDESS

The flowers of this attractive, characterful rose are medium-size and cupped in shape. The colour is a delicate, soft blush-pink with some light apricot tones. The fragrance is delicious and fruity, with a hint of lemon. This is a really strong growing rose which repeat-flowers very well. It makes a bushy, attractive-looking shrub with upright growth. The foliage is exceptionally large. To get the best from this rose, you must prepare the soil in advance of planting. Plenty of organic matter will encourage it to grow strongly and an annual mulch will also contribute to its overall wellbeing.

Shrub Rose | 2005
H: 90cm x S: 60cm

BALLERINA
(see page 86)

The flowers of 'Ballerina' have charm and simplicity. They are single, opening dark pink and fading quite quickly with age to a pale pink with a white centre. It provides excellent ground cover. The foliage is healthy and it has very few thorns. It makes a neat, bushy plant that can always be relied on for a good display. This classy rose is happy when grown in an open, sunny position. It only requires the lightest of pruning and does appreciate good soil conditions.

Hybrid Musk | 1937
H: 1.5m x S: 1.75m

CÉLESTE
(syn. *R.* x *alba* 'Celestial')

The origins of this beautiful rose are lost in time. Its cup-shaped, semi-double flowers are a soft pink and, when fully open, they reveal the golden stamens. The scent is strong and sweet and the foliage is an attractive grey-green colour and generally disease-free. This rose is happy to grow in shade and I find the flower colour holds well in a bright spot that's out of direct sunlight. It's an old rose that's worthy of care and attention and should be seen in gardens more frequently.

Hybrid Alba | 1759
H: 2m x S: 1.5m

CONSTANCE SPRY

If you're looking for a truly romantic rose, one that always jumps to mind is this one, bred by David Austin. The round, cabbage-rose-shaped flowers are a gorgeous warm pink, paler on the outside and deeper on the inside. The scent is powerful,  spicy and exotic. Sadly, it's not repeat-flowering but should be forgiven because its June display is fantastic. It can be grown as a lax shrub but, in my opinion, it is best trained as a climber against a sunny wall, where it will be covered from top to bottom in gorgeous blooms. Prune lightly if growing as a climber.

Shrub Rose | 1961
H: 2.5m x S: 1.5m

CORDELIA

Pretty shades of pink, ranging from purest rose-pink through to softer pink, characterise this rose. The long, shapely buds are particularly attractive. It makes a bushy, low-spreading plant with healthy foliage and a good display of loose, double flowers. These are cupped when open and are produced  in sprays. The petals have a silky quality. This rose is best grown in a sunny spot, sheltered from the wind and should be pruned lightly. It appreciates a well-drained soil and an annual mulch.

Shrub Rose | 2000
H: 1m x S: 1m

DUCHESSE D'ANGOULÉME

This sumptuous antique French rose produces full, double, mid- to pale-pink flowers, with tissue-paper-thin petals whose colour deepens towards the centre of the flower. In bright light, the edges of the petals can become ivory-white. The flower shape is round and globe-like and before the flower unfolds fully, the centre is roughly quartered. The flowers appear in clusters of three to five. This rose is not as tall as other Gallicas and produces very few thorns. This rose should be grown with great care. Make sure that the soil is fertile and the addition of mulch will help to keep in moisture in summer when the plant is producing flowers. It responds well to being grown in a sunny, sheltered spot.

Gallica | 1821
H: 1.25m x S: 1m

EGLANTYNE
(see page 102)

This is regarded as one of David Austin's most beautiful roses. The pink flowers are beautifully formed. It makes a medium-high, bushy plant with plenty of flowers that look particularly well when used as a specimen in mixed borders. The flowers have a delicate, old-rose fragrance. There are few problems with disease. Like many of David Austin's roses, it's also an excellent cut flower.

Shrub Rose | 1994
H: 1.5m x S: 1.25m

FANTIN-LATOUR
(see page 97)

This stunning rose flowers in June and produces fully double flowers which, when open, take on a flattish appearance. They are rose-pink and are produced in clusters. The fragrance is light and sweet. It's a good idea to prune the bush lightly just after flowering to maintain a good shape. This beautiful rose is best grown in a sunny, sheltered spot. It likes well-drained soil and appreciates regular feeding and mulching. It has generally good disease-resistance.

Modern Hybrid | 1940s
H: 1.75m x S: 2m

FELICIA
(see page 37)

Of all the Hybrid Musk roses available, 'Felicia' is well worth considering. Its double flowers are produced in clusters and open from shapely rose-pink buds to gorgeous pink flowers with apricot to salmon tones. Its growth is spreading. 'Felicia' can retain its overall shape very well with pruning, otherwise it makes a gently arching bush. It can look splendid when allowed to trail over low walls. It's best planted where there is plenty of sun and if you are growing it in a raised bed, it will need to be mulched to help retain moisture in the soil. The foliage is dark green with a slightly crinkled appearance.

Hybrid Musk | 1928
H: 1.5m x S: 1m

FÉLICITÉ PARMENTIER

It is believed that this rose is a hybrid between an Alba rose and a Damask. I love the flat, double flowers, each  with a button eye. The colour is a warm flesh-pink and, as the flowers age, they fade to pale pink and then to white. The profuse flowers usually appear in clusters of between three and eight. The growth is upright, stiff and dense. The leaves are attractive with a grey-blue tint. Though this is a once-flowering rose, it is one of the longest to bloom. It can be used as a low-growing hedge and is excellent for a semi-shaded position.

Alba Rose | 1834
H: 1.5m x S: 1m

FRITZ NOBIS
(see page 118)

This is a vigorous rose which is happy to grow on poor soil, but will respond best to good cultivation. Its buds are particularly shapely and the semi-double flowers open medium-pink with pale salmon tones, revealing a centre with golden-yellow stamens. The foliage is dark green and generally healthy. It's noted for having an attractive display of hips in winter.

Shrub Rose | 1940
H: 2m x S: 1.75m

GEOFF HAMILTON

This rose makes a large shrub with really strong growth. It produces great quantities of large chalice-shaped flowers which start warm pink in the centre, fading to the palest pink and almost white at the edges. The fruity scent is truly delicious. This rose repeat-flowers through the summer and into autumn and, if grown well, it's unusual to find it without flowers. It's excellent for cutting, and is particularly attractive as the buds unfold. It will grow in sun or light shade. The mid-green foliage is healthy and it has generally good disease-resistance, but keep an eye out for blackspot.

Shrub Rose | 1997
H: 1.5m x S: 1.25m

HERITAGE

This is a very popular English rose by David Austin. Its first flush is extremely free-flowering and is followed by more blooms throughout  the rest of the season, into autumn and even early winter. The flowers are a gorgeous pale salmon-pink and appear in clusters of three to seven. Wet weather can damage the opening bud and it's not the best cut flower as the petals are inclined to drop early. The foliage is dark green and glossy and generally healthy, but it can occasionally get attacked by blackspot. It is best grown in a bright spot out of direct sunlight, where you can appreciate the delicate and subtle shading of its magnificent flowers.

Shrub Rose | 1984
H: 1.2m x S: 1m

JAMES GALWAY
(see page 46)

The flowers on this rose are truly remarkable. Every petal is beautifully placed to make a glorious medium-sized domed flower. The colour is a rich warm pink, dark at the centre and fading to a glorious soft sugar-pink at the edges. It has a delicate old-rose fragrance. Grown against a wall, it makes a superb climber and can reach two and a half to three metres (one and a half when grown as a bush rose) in height. It is very disease-resistant and you can expect a good crop of flowers throughout the summer, as it repeats well. Good drainage is required. If you're growing it as a climber, only light pruning is needed. It's especially important to deadhead this rose.

Shrub Rose | 2000
H: 1.5m x S: 1m

KÖNIGIN VON DÄNEMARK
(syn. Queen of Denmark)

This gorgeous rose has large pink flowers, flat and very full-petalled, quartered on opening and with a central button eye. Its rich pink colouring has made it popular. The petals fade from a darker centre to a soft, pale pink outer edge. The scent is fantastic. The plant is  compact and produces dark green, healthy foliage. It's extremely thorny. A great rose, which can be used in a mixed border to add a touch of old-world charm.

Alba Rose | 1826
H: 1.5m x S: 1m

LOUIS VAN TYLE
(syn. 'Louis van Till')

A combination of exquisite colouring and delicious scent makes this rose desirable. The flowers are double and quartered with a central button eye that sometimes reveals golden yellow stamens. They are carried in clusters of between three and five and are a lilac mauve-pink with an outer sheath of paler pink petals. It is a once-flowering rose, giving a really good show. The foliage is mid-green and generally healthy. It needs good-quality soil if it's to flower well and give of its best. It isn't always widely available, but it is worth seeking out.

Gallica | < 1846
H: 1.5m x S: 1.25m

MADAME LOUIS LÉVÊQUE
(see page 98)

This is truly a great repeat-flowering Moss rose. It produces small clusters of large rose-pink flowers that develop a beautiful globular shape. They have a strong scent and are noted for keeping their colour. Though it's a Moss rose, the buds only show a very light covering of moss. It's strong and upright-growing, though not the ideal rose in rain, as it tends to ball (see page 182). It's at its best in sun and loves dry, warm weather. This rose benefits from a light pruning. It must have free-draining soil or it will suffer. It also does not like extremes of moisture or drought and so will benefit from an annual mulch.

Moss Rose | 1898
H: 1.5m x S: 1m

MADAME PIERRE OGER

This is a sport of 'La Reine Victoria' (see page 151) and, unusually for a sport, is more highly regarded than the original. The roses are identical in every way except for the colour. 'Madame Pierre Oger' has soft, clear-pink flowers sometimes tipped with crimson. The  blooms have a wonderfully delicate, translucent quality. The growth is upright but this rose has inherited a susceptibility to blackspot and mildew, which can cause problems for gardens in damp climates. This rose should not be pruned hard, but responds better to light pruning. It also benefits from being grown in best-quality, fertile soil.

Bourbon | 1872
H: 2m x S: 75c

SAINT SWITHUN
(see page 40)

An English rose that is noted for its exceptional myrrh-like fragrance. The flowers are large and of medium-pink when first opening, gradually maturing to a softer shade, the outer edges fading to white. The lightly cupped flowers are borne as single blossoms or in clusters of up to five. It repeat-flowers throughout the season and the growth is very thorny. The foliage is healthy and smooth with large grey-green leaves. I have found the colour of the flowers holds better in a slightly shady spot. Good drainage is needed, and regular feeding, especially after the first flush of flowers.

Shrub Rose | 1993
H: 1.5m x S: 1m

SCARBOROUGH FAIR

This is a soft pink rose of great charm, producing small, cup-shaped, informal-looking flowers with a centre of golden stamens. The medium-strong fragrance is good – fresh and green with old-rose sweetness. The flowers are semi-double and are produced in small sprays. It's very free-flowering, starting in early summer and continuing until late autumn. Short and compact in its growth, it makes a very attractive, neat, rounded plant. It's best positioned towards the front of a border where it's not overpowered by other plants.

Shrub Rose | 2003
H: 80cm x S: 60cm

STANWELL PERPETUAL
(see page 114)

This is a lovely old cottage-garden rose. The flowers are shell-pink and fade to white, opening out flat. It may get blackspot but, with good cultivation, this never really becomes a major problem. This rose may also take a while to establish. It's not good as a cut flower, as the petals drop quickly when in water. It only needs very light pruning.

Spinosissima | 1838
H: 2m x S: 1.5m

ALAN TITCHMARSH

Launched by Alan Titchmarsh at the Chelsea Flower Show in 2005, this is one of David Austin's finest recent introductions. The flowers are deeply cupped and very full with petals that are slightly incurved. The outer petals are pale pink and the inner ones are a richer, warmer pink shade. It produces its flowers in small groups – between three and four to a stem – and they have a typical old-rose fragrance with a hint of lemon. It grows as a large shrub with arching growth and, when established, it is a spectacular sight in full flower. I'm assured that it has good disease-resistance and I recommend planting it in groups of three or five for best impact.

English Rose | 2005
H: 1.2m x S: 90cm

BONICA
(see page 36)

This is a fabulous rose, producing semi-double, soft pink flowers which are softly scented. The foliage is rich green and it makes a compact, tidy plant. In full flower, it is a magnificent sight. It's happy if grown in sun or light shade. It appreciates a light pruning in winter and really responds well to mulching with an organic feed, such as home-made garden compost. The flowers are not very large but are produced in great quantity throughout the summer.

Shrub Rose | 1985
H: 1m x S: 1.25m

COMPLICATA
(see page 76)

'Complicata' is an elegant single-flowering rose that produces rich pink flowers with a central boss of golden stamens. The foliage is generally healthy and is mid- to pale green in colour. This rose is tolerant of relatively poor soil conditions and makes an excellent choice as an informal hedge. It can also be used as a climber and can grow upwards without the need of a trellis or support. It's a rose which is extremely easy to root from cuttings. 'Complicata' has excellent disease-resistance. It requires very little pruning and benefits from the application of a mulch while it is establishing.

Gallica
H: 2.5m x S: 1.5m

GLOIRE DES MOUSSEUSES

Regarded by many experts as possibly being the finest of all Moss roses, the beautiful colour and shapely, large pink flowers of 'Gloire des Mousseuses' have won this rose great acclaim. It has a delicious and powerful fruity scent, and though its petals fade gently in colour at the edges, the impact of each flower is of a clear, pure pink. Once established, it can produce clusters of between three and seven flowers per stem. The foliage is pale green and healthy. It's an excellent rose to consider as an informal hedge. The flowers also last reasonably well in water; it's worthwhile picking some in bud so you can appreciate their delicate mossy growth.

Moss Rose | 1852
H: 1.5m x S: 1.25m

JUBILEE CELEBRATION

One of David Austin's richly coloured English roses. The dome-shaped flowers are two-tone – shades of

dusky pink inside and tinges of yellow on the reverse of the petals – and the fragrance is rich and fruity. It has dark green, glossy foliage and the growth is strong and vigorous. This is a very healthy variety with good disease-resistance. It's also very reliable rose and repeat-flowers well.

Shrub Rose | 2002
H: 1.2m x S: 1.2m

LÉONARDO DE VINCI

This is a modern French shrub rose, raised by Meilland, but with lots of old-fashioned qualities. The rounded flowers are unusual – a combination of rich pink and apricot with underlying orange – and are fully double. They're produced in large clusters of between six and twelve. Glorious at their peak, sadly, as they fade and the petals drop, they take on some brown tones. This rose has little or no scent but flowers almost contin-uously and has a very romantic look. It is happiest in a

warm, sunny climate and is worth considering as a low-growing hedge that will give a colourful display.

Shrub Rose | 1994
H: 1m x S: 1m

MRS JOHN LAING
(see page 78)

This rose carries large, fully double pink flowers, with high outer and shorter inner petals, creating a beautiful goblet shape. The buds are particularly beautiful. It's a fabulous rose for cutting, as it lasts well in water and you can really appreciate the full beauty of its colouring at close quarters. It produces light green foliage and there is hardly a thorn to be found. The scent is exquisite, strong and sweet. 'Mrs John Laing' is a first-class rose. Be careful not to prune it too hard and pay careful attention to removing old or dead growth. It's never happy if grown in waterlogged soil so drainage is always important.

Hybrid Perpetual | 1887
H: 1.5m x S: 1.5m

RAUBRITTER
(see page 57)

This makes a bushy, sprawling plant that is ideal for growing over low walls. It can also be trained as ground cover. It's once-flowering but very profuse, and it has a slight fragrance. The flowers have a very distinctive globular appearance. 'Raubritter' is best planted in groups where you'll get a greater impact from the display. It can be prone to blackspot and mildew in some seasons, but I have found that extra generous cultivation by feeding well helps the plant to be somewhat more resilient. Although this rose likes dry conditions, it benefits from the application of a mulch to hold in moisture during dry summer weather.

Shrub Rose | 1936
H: 2.5m x S: 2.5m

SOUVENIR D'ADOLPHE TURC
(see page 99)

This charming rose produces semi-double flowers that fade gradually from palest coral to pink of varying shades. The combination is really gorgeous. It produces a tidy, neat plant and the large clusters of flowers are produced on arching stems. It has very few thorns and flowers continuously. Excellent for growing in containers, where it combines superbly with other plants in separate pots. It's a rose that benefits from a sunny, sheltered spot. It needs good drainage and regular feeding, especially if grown in a container.

Polyantha | 1924
H: 60cm x S: 80cm

THE COUNTRYMAN
(see page 86)

This has a real old-rose character with large, ruffled pink flowers, the centres of which are rich and glowing. They're produced in clusters and rosehips often follow in the autumn. However, this will encourage further blooms and you can expect it to flower until the first frost. The foliage is healthy and it can be grown along the ground, but you'll need to peg the stems down. For best results with The Countryman, position it in an open, sunny spot. It generally has good disease-resistance and will respond really well to being fed.

Shrub Rose | 1987
H: 1.25m x S: 2m

BOURBON QUEEN
(see page 79)

A magnificent old French rose, 'Bourbon Queen' has long been a favourite of cottage gardeners. The flowers, which are strong pink with a hint of purple and a white patch in the centre, appear in a main flush in June. They are cupped and the petals are crinkled and beautifully veined with dark shades of pink. The mid-green foliage is distinctly toothed and leathery. This rose benefits from good growing conditions, regular feeding and mulching. The autumn hips are very attractive.

Bourbon Rose | 1834
H: 1.75m (4m as a climber) x S: 1.5m

R. X CENTIFOLIA CRISTATA
(syn. 'Chapeau de Napoléon')

This rose has unique-looking buds that have crested growths and a moss-like appearance. It is commonly known as 'Winged Moss' and is sometimes called 'Cabbage Rose'. Its flowers can be borne singly or in clusters. They are large, with over a hundred petals, and are of the most

beautiful pure rose-pink. The scent is strong and sweet. It's a magnificent rose for cutting, looking like a flower plucked straight from an Old Master oil painting. The flowers last well in water but there is a real beauty about them as the petals begin to drop.

Centifolia | 1827
H: 1.5m x S: 1.5m

COMTE DE CHAMBORD
(syn. 'Madame Knorr')

One of the very best old-fashioned roses, its fully double flowers are

packed with petals and sometimes quartered. The colour is a rich, deep pink, occasionally splashed with hints of mauve. The flowers are cup-shaped, though the outer petals reflex, which adds to the full look of the flowers. The scent is a strong, typically heady old-rose perfume. The foliage is a mid- to soft-green and the stems are extremely prickly. It enjoys warm, sunny weather; the flower buds are inclined to 'ball' in a wet summer. I've seen this rose combined with peonies and it's a stunning sight.

Portland | 1860
H: 1.75m x S: 1.25m

FLOWER CARPET PINK
(see page 60)

This magnificent rose is appreciated for its healthy, strong growth, and makes an excellent ground cover rose. The small, usually semi-double flowers are a deep, rich pink, emerging from red buds. They appear in large clusters of up to twenty and each flower has a small white eye in the centre. There are different colour forms available. Flower Carpet benefits from being grown in full sun. The foliage is rich bright green and glossy. Only light pruning is required to keep the plant tidy.

Ground Cover Rose | 1989
H: 80cm x S: 1m

GERTRUDE JEKYLL

I adore the dark pink flowers of this David Austin rose. In bud, they are a soft crimson, gradually fading to paler shades of pink at the edges as they age. The large flowers are flat when fully open and the petals are sometimes quartered in the centre. The scent is exceptionally fine and it makes a good cut flower. It is a rose with great vigour. It can also be grown as a climber, when it will reach about three metres on a warm, sunny wall. Encourage repeat flowering by deadheading. Gertrude Jekyll responds well to being grown in a sunny, sheltered spot.

Shrub Rose | 1986
H: 1.25m x S: 1m

ISPAHAN
(see page 115)

An exceptionally good Damask rose, this is certainly one that should be in every collection. The fully double flowers are small in comparison with other Damasks and appear in clusters. Though only once-flowering, it lasts long enough to make an impact. The scent is strong and very sweet.

Damask Rose | 1832
H: 2m x S: 2m

JACQUES CARTIER
(syn. 'Marchesa Boccella')

This is a great shrub rose with double blooms of a rich, brilliant pink whose petals are slightly paler on the reverse. The light green foliage is the perfect foil to the blooms. Healthy and free-flowering, it does fantastically well in cold areas as it's extremely hardy. It also tolerates wet weather; rainwater simply runs off the petals. It repeat-

flowers well, producing a new flush of flowers every five to six weeks until the coldest weather sets in. The growth is narrow, upright and compact. It is suitable for growing in containers and may also be considered for an informal, low-growing hedge.

Portland Rose | 1868
H: 1.5m x S: 1m

JENNY DUVAL

The flower colouring of this old beauty is remarkable. Pink, mauve, grey, lilac, lavender and cerise all appear and melt together as it ages from bud to petal fall. The colours vary depending on the weather and

sometimes take on a bluish tone. It's a strong, vigorous rose. It can also be grown in a container. It is happy to grow in sun or light shade and it appreciates good quality, free-draining soil. Regular feeding and the addition of a mulch will always help to improve the growing quality of the bush.

Gallica | 1821
H: 1.25m x S: 1m

LA REINE VICTORIA

Beautiful, round, almost-spherical flowers characterise this rose. The colour is a delicate combination of

silvery pink and lilac, with deeper tones in the centre. The flowers are produced in attractive clusters of between three and nine, and its first flush is in early summer, with repeat-flowering well into autumn, though with far fewer flowers. The habit of this rose is upright and narrow and it's strong-growing with pale-green foliage. It's not particularly good at standing up to rain, which can make the buds ball (see page 182), and sadly, it's also susceptible to mildew and blackspot,

so it's a rose that's really suited to hotter, drier climates. I've tried this rose several times with varying success but, when in flower, she's so beautiful that I can't give her up.

Bourbon Rose | 1872
H: 2m x S: 75cm

LA VILLE DE BRUXELLES

This Damask rose stands out from the crowd. It's a strong, upright grower that produces magnificent large, double, quartered blooms on strong stems. The flowers are a deep rose-pink with a button eye, and they hold their colour well, only fading slightly at the edges as they age. As they open, they enlarge from a cup shape to an open, flat bloom. The fragrance is a powerful, sweet, old-rose scent. This rose has great character. If you can afford the space, plant in a group for impact. It definitely benefits from an annual mulch of well-rotted organic matter and I often use home-made garden compost, which I find makes a difference to its overall health.

Damask Rose | 1836
H: 1.75m x S: 1.5m

LOUISE ODIER

This is an old-fashioned rose of exceptional quality with beautiful flowers, fantastic scent and continuous flowering. A real 'must-have' rose. The flowers are fully double and an interesting combination of pink and lilac tones. They are produced in clusters and sit nicely on the bushy shrub. The foliage is light green and the stems are prickly and very vigorous. It's a hardy rose which really enjoys a sunny, sheltered corner where it can benefit from the warmth of walls on two sides. It repeat-flowers into early autumn.

Bourbon Rose | 1851
H: 1.5m x S: 1.2

MADAME ISAAC PEREIRE
(see page 18)

'Madame Isaac Pereire' is one of the most beautiful of Bourbon roses. You can grow it as a strong bush – it has an open, arching habit – in which case it makes an outstanding shrub in a mixed border in sun and free-draining soil. It is also equally good as a climber, making an excellent plant trained against a wall where it will reach approximately two and a half metres in height. The first blooms can be a little disappointing, as the flowers are occasionally disfigured, whereas the autumn flush is usually perfect as it seems to enjoy the cool, damp air of this season. The very double flowers are large and unravel in whirls of crimson and deepest pink. It is said that this rose grows well in poor soils but my belief is that if you want the best, you have to give it the best. It has good disease-resistance.

Bourbon Rose | 1881
H: 1.5m x S: 2m

MEVROUW NATHALIE NYPELS

(see page 93)

This is a rose with lots of old-world charm. It has long been popular and will give you a really good display of salmon-pink flowers that slowly fade to creamy white. The foliage is dark green and glossy and the plant's spreading growth makes a lovely shape. It's important to deadhead the flowers to prolong the display. It's extremely easy to root from cuttings and makes a lovely choice for a low-growing hedge. This splendid rose is happy in a sunny spot where it will give the best of its flowers. It requires light pruning and appreciates well-drained soil. It also benefits from regular feeding and mulching. It can be prone to a little disease but, with careful cultivation, this never becomes a problem.

Polyantha | 1919
H: 60cm x S: 75cm

PRÉSIDENT DE SÈZE

This rose is practically identical in form, shape and colouring to 'Jenny Duval' and some experts argue that they are one and the same. The buds open a crimson-pink and the flowers

contain a mixture of lilac, mauve, pink and magenta, with tones of grey and even a little violet. The flowers open out flat, showing off a centre massed with quilled petals. These are gathered and quartered around a green central eye. It is more thorny than most Gallica roses but is generally a healthy bush, which occasionally can suffer from blackspot. Position it in an open, sunny spot. The scent is soft and sweet.

Gallica | 1836
H: 1.25 x S: 1m

THE MAYFLOWER

This is an important English rose, bred by David Austin. The medium-sized, domed flowers have a simple charm and a beautiful, rich, old-rose fragrance. The growth is bushy and I like the way the flowers are carried well above the foliage. This is another one of David Austin's roses that really look splendid when grown in large groups. The flowers last well in water, making it an ideal choice as a rose for cutting. It benefits from being grown in a sunny, sheltered spot and responds well to regular feeding.

Shrub Rose | 2001
H: 1.2m x S: 1m

striped & bi-coloured

FERDINAND PICHARD

(see page 121)

'Ferdinand Pichard' originated in France in the early 1920s and is one of the best striped old roses you can grow. The flowers are pale pink with crimson stripes and splashes and they are produced in clusters. Their scent is strong and sweet. The foliage is light green and healthy. It's a strong-growing plant with good disease-resistance and, in a warm garden, it can be grown against a wall.

Hybrid Perpetual | 1921
H: 1m x S: 1.5m

HONORINE DE BRABANT

This attractive striped rose is great for a hot, sunny position. The flowers are cupped and the irregular crimson splashes and stripes are against a soft, pale pink background. As the flower matures, the background fades to white and the crimson turns to delicate violet-lilac. It's a strong, vigorous plant with really healthy foliage and very few prickles. This variety repeats well but you can expect its first flowering to be

the best, though it will carry flowers throughout the summer and well into autumn.

Bourbon Rose
H: 1.75m x S: 1.75m

LEDA

What is so special about this rose are the crimson buds that open to pure white, fully double flowers. These are tipped with crimson on the very outer edges of some but not all of the petals, creating a picotée effect. It's the contrast between the crimson and pure white which gives the flowers – produced in clusters of between three and five – a special presence in the garden. They also have a button eye, which adds a charming old-world look. This rose benefits

from being grown in a sheltered, sunny spot. Avoid a windy position. The shelter of surrounding plants can make all the difference to the quality of flower. It also benefits from being fed on a regular basis.

Damask Rose | 1827
H: 1.25m x S: 1.5m

VARIEGATA DI BOLOGNA
(see page 122)

This is my favourite striped rose. The flowers are palest rose-pink with crimson-purple stripes and flecks. In very hot gardens the stripes are paler, whereas in cooler gardens they're darker and the purple is more prevalent. The flowers appear in clusters of three to five on short stems. This rose is inclined to ball (see page 182) in wet weather and can be a little prone to blackspot. Good cultivation really helps, as does planting it in a sunny, sheltered spot.

Bourbon Rose | 1909
H: 3m x S: 2m

green

R. X ODORATA VIRIDIFLORA
(see page 123)

This real green rose is a sport of 'Old Blush'. It's more a curiosity than a flower of great beauty and is always a talking point in my garden where I've grown it against a north-facing wall for over twenty years. There it has reached a height of over two metres, but if you grow it as a bush it will be shorter. It is continuously in flower. 'Viridiflora' is of value to flower arrangers and looks super in a vase with other roses.

China Rose | 1845
H: 1m x S: 80cm

climbers and ramblers

This group of roses is valuable for adding colour to walls, fences, pergolas and arches. It contains a wide range of colours and flower types. With careful selection you can choose those that will provide interest to your garden from early summer until late autumn.

white-cream

ALBÉRIC BARBIER
(see page 48)

This rambling rose is an excellent choice for a shady spot. Its rich yellow buds open into creamy white flowers and the fragrance is strong and delicious. The foliage is green and glossy. It flowers from the middle of June and you can expect, with a little feeding, an excellent flush later in the season. One of the other great things about this rose is its tolerance for poor-quality soil, but it's important to make sure that the soil is free-draining. It benefits from being mulched, especially if grown in a warm, sunny spot, as this will help to retain moisture during the summer.

Rambler | 1921
H: 5m x W: 3.5m

BOBBIE JAMES
(see page 117)

This is a super rambler, happy to grow in sun or light shade, with an absolutely spectacular once-off flowering in the middle of summer. The strongly musk-scented flowers are small and produced in large clusters. They are lightly double and are white, flushed pink. When established, it makes a plant of up to five metres, so

it needs plenty of space. The autumn and winter hips are orange-red.

Multiflora Rambler | 1961
H: 5m x S: 3m

LAMARQUE

'Lamarque' is happiest in a warm climate. It makes a fabulous rambler and gives its best display in spring, though it continues to flower through the summer months, albeit less abundantly. Each flower is a double white pompon, opening ivory-white and gradually fading to purest white, and each is made up of a mass of small petals. The flowers are

produced in great abundance in clusters of three to four per stem and they have a rich, light tea-like scent that drifts on the air. It produces very few thorns and its foliage is generally disease-resistant.

Tea-Noisette | 1830
H: 5m x S: 3m

LONG JOHN SILVER

A really attractive rambler, not thanks to its growth, which is long, nor its habit, which is rather awkward-

looking, but because of its exquisitely beautiful flowers. Pure white and fully double, they

appear in large clusters of between six and twelve. The scent is sweet and musky. This rose needs a strong support: it is best grown against a wall in a sunny, sheltered spot. Prune lightly. Keep an eye out for blackspot, which this rose can be prone to.

Setigera Hybrid | 1934
H: 5m x S: 3m

MADAME ALFRED CARRIÈRE
(see page 26)

The strongly scented double flowers of this rambling rose are small and produced in clusters of between three and twelve. The flowers open from cream buds to ivory-white. This is an excellent rose to grow on a north-facing wall, where it will flower continuously throughout the summer. It really is non-stop. Pruning is really carried out just to keep the plant tidy.

Noisette | 1879
H: 5m x S: 2m

ALISTER STELLA GRAY
(see page 33)

The flowers open a deep buff and fade to white. They have an attractive button eye which adds great charm to the flowers. The foliage is small, dark green and glossy, and can sometimes be susceptible to blackspot and mildew. The flowers appear in clusters that can carry as many as thirty.

Noisette | 1894
H: 5m x S: 2m

AVIATEUR BLÉRIOT
(see page 85)

This is an old-fashioned rambling rose that I've seen used in Europe as a weeping standard. The colour of the flowers is warm and inviting. It's a lovely buff orange-yellow, paling to cream and white, and the flowers are double. It has an especially wonderful fragrance. This rose needs a sunny, sheltered spot. It can be prone to blackspot, so good soil cultivation is important, along with regular feeding.

Wichurlana Rambler | 1910
H: 4m x W: 2m

R. BANKSIAE 'LUTEA'
(see page 50)

This is a true garden classic. The double yellow flowers are borne in profusion and hang in sprays during April and May. They are a lovely golden creamy yellow. It has a reputation for being a little tender so is best grown in a warm sheltered spot where it can be protected from early frosts. It can reach great heights and is suitable for growing against a house or even up into a tree. Careful pruning is needed, the aim being to train the plant and prevent sections

becoming overcrowded. I'm always reluctant to overfeed this plant, as this can produce soft growth which can be damaged by frost in spring. The foliage colour is medium to light green and acts as a lovely foil to the clusters of small double flowers.

Wild Rose | 1824
H: 10m x S: 3m

MARÉCHAL NIEL

This climber is reputed to have been the favourite rose of Queen Victoria. The flowers are carried on weak stems, which, in a climbing rose, is an advantage as the flowers hang. They are a mixture of pale lemon-yellow to cream with some occasional apricot shades towards the centre. It's a rose that fades quickly. The foliage is pale green and the stems are quite prickly. Ideally suited to warmer gardens, it needs shelter and warmth outside,

and in northern gardens it requires the protection of a conservatory or greenhouse. Given the right conditions, it is spectacular in full bloom, covered in hanging, strongly scented blossoms.

Noisette | 1864
H: 4m x S: 3m

FORTUNE'S DOUBLE YELLOW
(syn. R. x odorata 'Pseudindica')

This rose has great character and charm and was originally brought back from China by Robert Fortune, an English plant hunter. When it's

happy, it must rank as one of the most free-flowering of all roses. The flowers are a blend of cream and pink with pale peach and honey-yellow. When it's in full flower, the massed effect of the small clusters of three to five blooms is spectacular. It has hooked, particularly vicious, thorns. It really enjoys a warm sunny spot and some of the best plants I've seen in Ireland are in cold conservatories which give winter protection and an extra boost of heat in summer. It's interesting to note that it had disappeared from cultivation and was reintroduced to Britain from an old garden near Dublin.

China Rose | 1845
H: 3m x S: 4m

GOLDEN SHOWERS
(see page 28)

The buds of this modern climbing rose are exceptionally attractive as they open to large, double flowers of a rich, bright yellow colour. The blooms are good for cutting and the rich green foliage is attractive but can sometimes be susceptible to blackspot and mildew. This rose is noted for being particularly good for standing up to wet weather. It also is good for light shade, though the flowers may appear later in this situation. It's a super rose for a small garden as it never gets too big and it's also tidy and really easy to keep under control. It is, however, inclined to make bushy, rather than climbing, growth so careful training is needed and it's important to have secure trellis or support to attach it to. As the growth is strong and upright, I have found that it can grow away from the wall. Therefore, careful pruning is required to train it so that it grows along the wall instead.

Modern Climber | 1956
H: 3m x S: 2m

LEVERKUSEN

This is a hardy climbing rose with an abundance of semi-double flowers, egg-yolk yellow in the centre, shading  outwards to sulphur-yellow. The scent is medium and not exceptionally strong, though it is sweet. In cooler countries you'll get one main flush followed by a lesser, but, nonetheless continuous display. In warmer countries it will produce several very full flushes. It's a strong-growing climber that really enjoys a warm sheltered spot. It needs good support and is excellent for growing on pergolas and trellises. It can be prone to blackspot, which must be treated early.

Kordesii | 1954
H: 3m x S: 2m

MERMAID
(see page 27)

This famous rose has soft primrose-yellow single flowers and a light fragrance. It can be slow to establish but in time it will make a formidable plant, so you need to give it plenty of space if you are to appreciate its full beauty. It needs shelter while it is getting established, as young or newly-planted specimens are vulnerable to frost. When it's happy, it's fast growing. It's best planted in a sheltered spot and tolerates shade, but it is a rose that is happiest when it's warm.

Bracteata Hybrid | 1918
H: 5m x S: 4m

CLIMBING LADY HILLINGDON

The new growth and young foliage of this magnificent climbing rose is an attractive copper-purple colour, which complements the colour of the flowers extremely well. These are a rich apricot, darker at the centre, with some hints of amber, buff and honey. They fade gently as they mature, with the petals turning ivory and cream at the edges. The buds are exquisite – long and shapely – and in the summer season, when established, this rose is constantly flowering, producing its beautiful blooms in clusters of three to five. These hang, making it easy to appreciate them as you look up into  them. I find that they last exceptionally well in water. This is a vigorous climber and I have seen it growing in many Irish gardens, where it does best on sheltered, south-facing walls.

Tea Rose | 1917
H: 4m x S: 2m

ALCHYMIST

If you're looking for a climbing rose with an unbelievably rich fragrance, this is one. Its scent can only be described as near-intoxi-cating. Sadly, this rose isn't as  widely available as it should be. The flowers are large and fully double and the colouring is a combination of copper, pink and orange-yellow – the colour of ripe mangoes and apricots. The foliage is a rich green and has good disease-resistance. It's not the best rose for continuous flowering but this is something I forgive it for because of the quality and fragrance of the blooms.

Modern Hybrid | 1956
H: 4m x W: 3m

AUGUSTE GERVAIS

This rose is a wonderful rambler but is more often grown as a weeping standard. Its semi-double blooms open initially a copper-yellow and, as they mature, they change to ivory-white. The flowers repeat well through the summer and the fragrance is pleasant and sweet. The foliage is dark green, providing an excellent contrast against the flowers. It's magnificent when grown as a specimen plant, when you can appreciate its full glory.

Wichuriana | 1918
H: 5m x W: 1m

BREATH OF LIFE
(syn. 'Harquanne')

This shrub rose is happy to climb when it's got a support and it's often sold and grown as a climber. I grow it for its gorgeous colouring – a combination of apricot and soft coral-pink. The fragrance is medium-sweet with an underlying muskiness and it's particularly popular with flower arrangers, as it holds well as a cut flower. You can expect a vigorous, upright plant but if you grow it as a bush, expect it to be somewhat lanky with a bare bottom. So it's a good idea to have some planting around it for disguise.
Providing you maintain good soil fertility, low-growing shrubs and perennials are suitable. Just remember, its  exquisite colouring will give you opportunities for some attractive colour combinations.

Shrub Rose | 1980
H: 2m x S: 1.25m

BUFF BEAUTY

I've grown this most popular of the Hybrid Musks for nearly thirty years and would never be without it. It has exquisite colouring – yellow and apricot with buff, ivory and honey – attractively shaped flowers and a  strong, sweet scent. The colour varies; I believe it's due to climate as, in cooler weather, the shade deepens whereas in warmer, hot spells, the tones are soft and lighter. The growth is lax and I grow it as a low climber. The young foliage is copper-coloured, turning to dark green. It's an easy-to-grow rose that's healthy and vigorous, giving several flushes of flowers throughout the season, especially in early autumn. In mild spots, it has been known to flower into winter. It has excellent disease-resistance.

Hybrid Musk | 1939
H: 2m x S: 1.5m

CLIMBING MRS SAM MCGREDY

This climbing sport of 'Mrs Sam McGredy' repeat-flowers well. It produces large, semi-double flowers and is extremely early-flowering – it's one of the first climbing roses to bloom. The reverse of each petal is flushed red, and the centre and gradually folding petals are a combination of peach, apricot and orange. The colour changes as the rose develops. The flowers don't last long but there are always new ones, especially if you deadhead. This rose isn't always widely available as it can be difficult to propagate, but it's worth searching for as it's top-class and very free-flowering.

Hybrid Tea | 1937
H: 3m x S: 1.75

GÉNÉRAL SCHABLIKINE
(see page 96)

This rose is seldom out of flower. Exquisite blooms of a remarkable colour open from shapely scrolled buds. The flowers are a combination of pink, copper, orange and red. It has a light and delicate tea scent which is delicious. It makes an upright, bushy plant and can also be grown as a climber against a wall. The foliage is healthy and it appreciates rich growing conditions. It likes an open, sunny position and benefits from light pruning. The soil should be well drained. It can be prone to blackspot.

Tea Rose | 1878
H: 1.75m x S: 1.25m

GLOIRE DE DIJON
(see page 112)

A climbing rose of great character, 'Gloire de Dijon' carries richly scented, fully double buff-coloured flowers. It needs good cultivation if you're to get the best from it. The foliage is attractive but there can be problems with blackspot. It really responds to a sheltered, sunny spot.

Climbing Tea | 1853
H: 5m x S: 3m

MAIGOLD
(see page 74)

Semi-double, loosely-formed flowers with a good fragrance, in shades of orange, bronze and yellow, which appear early in the season, make this rose a 'must-have'. It's one of the best early-flowering climbers you can grow. The stems are exceptionally thorny and it is strong-growing with good disease-resistance. It will happily grow in poor soil but, as with any rose it will respond well to feeding. Take great care when pruning this rose as it is extremely thorny so it's important to wear protective gloves. 'Maigold' benefits from a mulch and the soil should be well drained.

Shrub Rose | 1953
H: 3m x S: 1.5m

MEG

This climbing rose has an unusually open flower exposing the central boss of stamens. Its colour is exceptional – a delicate combination of amber-yellow,  peach and pink, with rust tones towards the centre. The petals are darker on the reverse. As the flower matures, it fades to a soft pale pink. The scent is light and fresh. The flowers are produced on long stems in clusters of five to ten. It's a lanky-growing plant with very stiff, upright growth; the wood is so hard to bend that it's not ideal for growing on an arch or pergola. Its best grown against a sunny wall, although you might like to try it as a tall, freestanding shrub.

Modern Climber | 1954
H: 3m x S: 1.5m

PAUL TRANSON
(see page 58)

This is a delightful Wichuriana rose with small double flowers, which are the most beautiful salmon-pink with copper and orange tones. They have a delicious scent. It's free-flowering, continuing into autumn, when the crop of flowers often increases. It has generally good disease-resistance and appreciates regular feeding and the application of a mulch. I tend to use home-made garden compost for this, which it seems to adore. Best grown in a sunny spot in free-draining soil.

Wichuriana Rambler | 1900
H: 4m x S: 2.5m

CLIMBING ÉTOILE DE HOLLANDE
(see page 29)

This climbing version has larger flowers than the bush rose. The buds are beautifully formed and open to rich velvety crimson flowers with a strong, sweet fragrance. It's a good repeat-flowerer. It's happy growing in a bright spot out of direct sunlight and it also tolerates shade – in fact the flowers look better in a shady spot – but avoid heavy shade. The growth is very upright but it can become lanky and bare at the base, so it's a good idea to have some companion planting to conceal this. The foliage can also be sparse so you might consider planting some late-flowering clematis with it. The flowers are very good for cutting and last well in water.

Climbing Hybrid Tea | 1931
H: 4m x S: 2.5m

DORTMUND
(see page 20)

An excellent low-growing climber that's easy to control and so is perfect for smaller gardens. The single, bright cherry-red flowers with white centres are really showy. These flowers are produced in clusters of between five and twelve. If you avoid deadheading, they are followed by a splendid crop of rich orange rosehips. The foliage is strong, dark and very healthy. In general, this rose to have very good disease-resistance. It grows equally well in sun or shade and in my own garden it grows on an east-facing wall. 'Dortmund' needs to be lightly pruned and, for best effect, should be trained carefully onto a support.

Kordesii Hybrid | 1955
H: 2m x S: 1.5m

CHEVY CHASE

This is a fantastic rambler, producing clusters of ten to twenty small, dark red double flowers whose colour turns to a bright cherry-red as they mature. It's extremely profuse in its flowering, and has pale green foliage that's much healthier than in other ramblers. It's moderately vigorous and may take a little while to settle in, but with time  it will make a large plant. It should be seen more often. I've planted it in my own garden in light shade, where it has settled in and is growing well. It needs a strong support to climb on.

Multiflora Rambler | 1939
H: 5m x S: 3m

CLIMBING CRIMSON GLORY

Raised in America, this glorious red climbing rose is noted for producing one spectacular show of flowers and then giving an intermittent display for the rest of the season. Its wonderful colour is matched by its very strong, sweet fragrance. The flowers are rich, brilliant crimson and as the petals unfold you find darker markings towards the edges. The blooms hang their heads which means you can appreciate them better as you look up. To get the best display, give it a south-facing wall in an open spot. It can be prone to blackspot and mildew but extra cultivation care should help to keep it healthy.

Hybrid Tea | 1935
H: 2.5m x S: 1.5m

DANSE DU FEU

Always popular, when this climbing red rose is happy and established, it

repeat-flowers well into the autumn after a fabulous initial flush. The semi-double flowers are a bright vermilion-red and are produced in clusters of between five and seven. It is a strong grower and needs a secure support. I'm particularly fond of the new foliage which is bronze-tinged early in the season. This rose flowers best when grown in a sunny position. It needs light pruning to keep it in shape and benefits from annual mulching.

Modern Climber | 1953
H: 3m x S: 2m

DUBLIN BAY

When I first saw this rose I was taken with its showiness, but disappointed that it has little or no scent. Despite this, it's incredibly popular. Its buds are a dark, deep red, opening to brilliant, rich velvety scarlet. The blooms are produced in clusters on long stems and it repeat-flowers

throughout the summer. It can be slow to establish but once it settles in, you'll be guaranteed a fabulous display. It's fast growing and hardy. If it had a scent, there'd be few others that could compare. It may be prone to a little blackspot, which should be treated with a proprietary fungicide. This rose

benefits from regular feeding and appreciates a mulch.

Modern Climber | 1974
H: 3m x S: 2m

GUINÉE
(see page 22)

To get the best from this fabulous climbing rose, you'll need to feed it well. I've grown it for many years and have learned the hard way – neglect it and it gets very unhappy, but care for it well and it flourishes. It has a strongly scented Hybrid Tea-shaped flower the colour of darkest scarlet. It's a fairly lanky-growing rose and the stems at the base of the plant can look quite ugly, so I recommend masking these with other plants. However, be careful that they don't compete with the rose; it isn't happy to share its root space and is likely to sulk. It can also get blackspot but, despite these faults, it's worth every effort to grow this stunning, sweetly scented, deepest red climbing rose.

Climber | 1938
H: 3.5m x S: 2.5m

SÉNÉGAL
(see page 16)

Raised in France by Mallerin in 1944, the flowers of this rose are so dark that they appear almost black. It is a seedling of the famous red climbing rose 'Guinée' and has a Hybrid Tea style of flower. These are small and are not produced in great quantity but their scent is rich, heavy and sweet. One cut rose can fill a room with its aroma. It repeat-flowers well and can reach a height of about five metres. It's best to grow it out of direct sunlight, as too much sun will scorch the delicate petals and turn them brown, but it does appreciate a bright spot. Despite this drawback, it is

worth every effort to secure this rose if you're looking for one with exceptional fragrance.

Climber | 1944
H: 5m x S: 3m

SOUVENIR DU DOCTEUR JAMAIN
(see page 17)

If ever a rose could be called greedy, this one is top of the list. I've seen it looking miserable and starved when growing in poor conditions, but in good-quality, rich soil and with regular feeding, the display of deep crimson, velvety flowers is exceptional. The buds are almost black and when the flowers open, the central stamens are exposed, showing a slight flash of gold. It has a heady, sweet scent to match its richness of colour. It grows remarkably well on a shaded wall and, although it is prone to blackspot and mildew, I have found that good cultivation can help to overcome this.

Hybrid Perpetual | 1865
H: 3m x S: 2.5m

SUPER EXCELSA
(syn. 'Helexa')

This is the improved version of the old rambler 'Excelsa'. The flowers are a rich carmine-crimson and are produced in large clusters. As the colour fades, it takes on a purple tone. It repeat-flowers well and produces healthy foliage. Super Excelsa is not as vigorous as 'Excelsa' and can be used as a low climber or shrub. I've seen it grown as a pillar rose where it looked super. It also makes a fabulous weeping standard. It can get a little mildew but this is usually late in the season and is easily dealt with.

Wichuriana Shrub | 1986
H: 2m x S: 2m

BLEU MAGENTA
(see page 121)

This exquisitely coloured rose is a rather curious shade of crimson and purple. The foliage is also attractive, but can be prone to mildew if it's too dry, so plant it in rich, well-cultivated, moisture-retentive soil. There are very few thorns on the branches, making it an excellent choice for pillars or large arches.

Multiflora Rambler | 1920
H: 4m x S: 2m

VEILCHENBLAU
(see page 43)

This is probably the best-known purple-flowered rambling rose. It's stunning, especially when grown over arches or on pergolas. It is thornless and is a very vigorous grower. The small double flowers are produced in clusters. It needs a sunny aspect and, ideally, should be planted in soil that is well drained. It benefits from mulching and good feeding. Pruning is required to prevent the plant becoming top heavy. Thinning the upper growth may be necessary when this rose is established.

Multiflora Rambler | 1909
H: 3m x S: 2m

ASH WEDNESDAY
(syn. 'Aschermittwoch')
(see page 120)

This is a beautiful rose with a difference, the difference being its unusually coloured flowers. These are an attractive washed lilac-pink and are produced in clusters of two to twelve. It only flowers once in the season. It makes a vigorous climber that produces lots of thorns. It may need some attention for blackspot.

Modern Climbing Rose | 1955
H: 5m x W: 2

BLUSH NOISETTE
(syn. 'Noisette Carnée')

I love this rose grown as a small climber, though it's usually seen as a shrub. The attractively formed double flowers repeat well and are produced in large clusters of twenty to fifty. The crimson buds open to soft lilac-pink flowers held on long stems. The fragrance is strong with a  distinctive spicy clove scent. The foliage is dark green. This rose can be slow to establish but, once it has settled in, it will be strong-growing and vigorous. It has excellent disease-resistance and is a rose I can highly recommend.

Noisette | 1817
H: 2.5m x S: 1.5m

BLUSH RAMBLER
(see page 106)

This is one of the most beautiful of the Multiflora ramblers. The flowers open bright pink, fading to a blush white, and are semi-double. Unfortunately, they can be marked by rain. The foliage is pale green and there are very few thorns. Its growth is vigorous. It does particularly well in warm climates.

Multiflora Rambler | 1903
H: 4m x S: 3m

CLIMBING CÉCILE BRÜNNER
(see page 51)

Delightfully formed, perfect miniature Hybrid Tea flowers are produced by this enchanting rose. In its climbing form, it is very vigorous and can reach great heights. The flowers appear in great profusion in June, after which you can expect fewer. They are small and dainty, which makes them useful for posies. This rose is generally disease-resistant and makes an imposing plant when established. I have found that regular mulching with well-rotted farmyard manure in my own garden has made a difference to the quality of this plant. It flowers happily in sun or shade but the best display has been on a plant I have grown in a sunny, sheltered corner.

Polyantha | 1894
H: 7m x S: 7m

CLIMBING DEVONIENSIS

To get the very best out of some roses you need to feed them well and this is definitely one of them. It needs good-quality soil and plenty of organic matter. The flowers start as pale pink buds, but open to a delicious creamy white with just a hint of pink plus honey tones at the centre. The many layers of petals roll back in the fully double flower. It has strongly scented flowers, sweet with a hint of tea. It likes a sunny, sheltered spot.

Tea Rose | 1858
H: 4m x S: 2m

CLIMBING OLD BLUSH

Definitely a rose that has stood the test of time, this is the climbing version of 'Old Blush China', which was introduced by Parson in 1789. The climber is more vigorous than the bush rose. Fragrant globular flowers open to semi-double rich pink blooms and are produced in clusters. These

flowers fade to a blush pink as they mature. I love their shape. This is a rose that should really be planted in a warm, sheltered spot and a little extra care should also be taken with soil preparation before planting. Regular feeding and an annual mulch help to keep the rose in healthy condition.

China Rose | 1789
H: 4.5m x S: 3m

CLIMBING SOUVENIR DE LA MALMAISON

Irish weather conditions are a little too damp for this rose – the flowers don't stand up to heavy rain – so I'm thinking of growing it in a cold conservatory. When grown well, it's one of the most beautiful of all roses. The flat, quartered flowers in soft blush-pink with shades of ivory have a strong, sweet fragrance. When grown outside, it's best positioned in a warm, sheltered, sunny spot. A

sunny corner would be ideal. It needs good-quality, free-draining, fertile soil. It can be a little prone to blackspot, so it is best to treat this early in the season to prevent it getting a hold.

Bourbon Climber | 1893
H: 3.5m x S: 2.5m

THE GENEROUS GARDENER
(see page 63)

The flowers of this important rose are a pale shell-pink, fading to almost white. They have a really attractive cup shape and a delicious fragrance. The Generous Gardener can be grown either as a shrub or a climber. It's a strong-growing rose and I have found that it makes an excellent climber with good disease-resistance. Light pruning is needed to keep a good shape and it is important to deadhead this rose. It benefits from regular feeding and appreciates being mulched with well-rotted organic matter such as farmyard manure, if available.

Shrub Rose | 2002
H: 3.6m x S: 2m

soft pink

ALBERTINE
(see page 54)

The delicious, strong scent of this old-fashioned rambling rose makes it indispensable and I have used it extensively in my garden-design work. The shapely buds are rich salmon pink and the fully open flowers are shades of orange, apricot and coral. It is very reliable and, although it can be prone to blackspot and mildew, is still worth growing: good cultivation can overcome these problems. Plant in a sunny spot and prune carefully to prevent it becoming top heavy.

Wichuriana Rambler | 1921
H: 6m x S: 4.5m

AWAKENING (syn. 'Probuzení')
(see page 113)

I put this rose high on my list of 'must-haves'. It's a gorgeous, fully double version of 'New Dawn' (see page 163) with warm, glowing pink apricot flowers that are produced over a long period. The flowers have a pleasant, sweet fragrance. This rose doesn't enjoy excessively wet weather and is excellent against a sunny wall. It can be susceptible to blackspot.

Climber | 1988 (reintroduction)
H: 3m x S: 2.5m

BALTIMORE BELLE
(see page 64)

A rambling rose noted for its late flowering season. Beautiful, palest flesh-pink flowers open from reddish buds. The flowers are fully double and gradually fade to an ivory-white colour, eventually turning pure white. They are produced in magnificent clusters. Foliage is fresh green and the growth is strong. It appreciates free-draining, good-quality soil and is fairly disease-resistant. Mulching and feeding help the plant with its summer display.

Setigera Hybrid | 1843
H: 4m x S: 3m

BLAIRII NUMBER TWO
(see page 65)

The large blooms of this rose are beautiful, not only in their neat shape but also for their lovely colouring – pink at the edges and often with lilac, grey and white towards the centre. It can sometimes be a tall, lanky-growing plant and can be susceptible to blackspot and mildew, but when you see it with its clusters of large, scented flowers, you'll be blown away.

Hybrid China | 1835
H: 3m x S: 2m

CLIMBING LADY SYLVIA

If you're looking for a strong-growing, upright rose – and one that doesn't ramble – I can recommend 'Climbing Lady Sylvia'. It's a sport of 'Climbing Madame Butterfly' (see below), boasting superb large blooms with rich pink centres and outer petals fading to blush-pink. It has a rich fragrance and repeat-flowers well. The thorny growth is stiff and upright.

Climbing Hybrid Tea | 1933
H: 4.5m x S:

CLIMBING MADAME BUTTERFLY

This is a beautiful scented rose in varying shades of pink with a soft lemon-coloured centre. The combination of its colouring and scent make it almost good enough to eat. It

forms a strong, vigorous climber. The flowers last well in water, making them very suitable for cutting. I have seen this rose grown against a wall in a lean-to greenhouse, to encourage early flowers to develop, which were then used for cutting. It's best grown in a sunny, sheltered spot. Pruning is necessary to keep a tidy shape against the wall.

Climbing Hybrid Tea | 1926
H: 4.5m x S: 3m

CLIMBING OPHELIA

Beautifully shaped buds open to rich, flesh-pink, highly fragrant flowers in this climbing form of one of the most beautiful early Hybrid Teas. It repeat-flowers well and it is noted for its good disease-resistance. It has excellent foliage. It is the same as 'Climbing Lady Sylvia' (see left) and 'Climbing Madame Butterfly' (see left) in all but colour.

Climbing Hybrid Tea | 1920
H: 4.5m x S: 3m

DEBUTANTE
(see page 67)

An excellent rambling rose – one of the best of its type – 'Debutante' produces an abundance of clear rose-pink flowers that gradually fade to a soft creamy pink. It has good disease-resistance and makes an excellent cut flower, as it adds an old-world look to flower arrangements. It needs the strong support that can be provided by an archway or pergola. Pruning is needed to keep the plant tidy. It's happy when grown in a sunny spot with free-draining soil.

Wichuriana Rambler | 1902
H: 5m x S: 3m

DOCTOR W. VAN FLEET
(see page 52)

If you've got the space, I recommend you grow this rambler with its large clusters of double, flesh-pink, sweetly scented flowers. It is a very vigorous grower and is noted for its dark green foliage and strong thorns. It is excellent for growing into trees. For the best display of flowers, you really need to grow this rose in sunshine, though I have seen it growing in some shade and doing very well. 'Doctor W. Van Fleet' can be prone to some

blackspot but with good cultivation, disease can be managed on this gorgeous rose. I'm particularly fond of the flower buds which are very shapely. They open to semi-double flowers. It responds well to feeding.

Wichuriana Rambler | 1910
H: 6m x S: 3.5m

DREAM GIRL

'Dream Girl' is a charming and very beautiful rose. The small, fully double flowers glow a gorgeous coral-pink that fades gradually as they open. The old-rose scent is penetrating and delicious and the flowers have an old-fashioned appearance to match – they are often quartered just as they open. The foliage is dark green and glossy. Usually flowering after midsummer, it is ideal for growing on trellis and excellent as a pillar rose. This rose grew very well in my mother's garden for many years where it gave a magnificent display each summer. It enjoys a sunny, sheltered spot.

Climber | 1944
H: 3m x S: 2m

FÉLICITÉ PERPÉTUE
(see page 49)

This is one of the best rambling roses that you can grow. It produces huge clusters of rose-cream to soft pink-white flowers. The buds start out crimson and change to become tinted shell-pink. The growth is strong and healthy and, when established, it will form a dense network of branches. The fragrance is sweet and delicate. The small flowers have an attractive shape; they are informally double, made up of many petals, and appearing in drooping clusters. The foliage is rich, glossy green and the overall plant is lacking in thorns. This is a rose which responds well to feeding.

With mulching and occasional feeding through the growing season, it helps to keep the plant in tip-top condition.

Sempervirens Hybrid | 1828
H: 5m x S: 3m

MADAME GRÉGOIRE STAECHELIN
(syn. 'Spanish Beauty')

I think the name 'Spanish Beauty' is very appropriate for this rose; it conjures up an image of a Spanish señorina holding an almost thornless bloom between her teeth. It's  such a good rose, my only regret is that it doesn't flower the entire summer, only in early summer. It has large, full, very fragrant, rich pink flowers, with soft pink edges to the petals as the flowers open. It's a strong, sturdy grower and also produces attractive rosehips.

Climbing Hybrid Tea | 1927
H: 4.5m x S: 3m

NEW DAWN

This rose – a famous sport of 'Doctor W. Van Fleet' (see left) – is popular in Irish gardens, and rightly so. I find myself recommending it time and time again when I'm asked for a rambler that offers value for money. The flowers are semi-double and soft  pink with an attractive light fragrance. It's noted for its continuous flowering. If you had space for just one rambler, 'New Dawn' is

the one. It will grow in sun or partial shade and is happy in most garden soils, but benefits from an annual mulch of well-rotted organic matter. Deadheading encourages a longer flowering period.

Wichuriana Rambler | 1930
H: 3m x S: 2.5m

PAUL'S HIMALAYAN MUSK

This is another great rambler for growing through trees and is considered one of the most beautiful and best. Soft blush to lilac-pink flowers appear in sprays. The flowers are fragrant. As an extra bonus, I find that it creates a thorny tangle, which is useful as added security in the garden. The thorns are broad and hooked, making them fierce to deal with. This is a rose that benefits from  good feeding. You can always expect a spectacular display of blooms in July.

Moschata | 19th century
H: 12m x S: 4.5m

PIERRE DE RONSARD
(syn. Eden Rose 88)
(see page 103)

The flowers on this continuous-flowering rose have a real old-fashioned look about them. They are beautifully formed, fully double and take several days to open from bud. The colour is a gorgeous shade of medium pink paling to cream at the edges. It has very few thorns and generally doesn't suffer from disease. One of the most best climbers I know.

Shrub Rose | 1987
H: 3m x S: 2m

SPIRIT OF FREEDOM

The stunning flowers of this rose, resembling smaller versions of those of 'Constance Spry', are deeply cupped and packed full of petals. The flowers are also quartered and are a soft, light pink which turns to lilac-pink as they age. The fragrance is delicious with undertones of myrrh. The healthy foliage is also very good with a grey-green sheen. It can be grown as a shrub or a climber; if grown as a shrub, it's best to plant in a group of three to five, depending on the available space. Alternatively, it makes an attractive sight grown against a wall.

Climber | 2002
H: 2.75m x S: 2.4m

bright mid-pink

CLIMBING MADAME CAROLINE TESTOUT
(see page 30)

This is a great favourite of mine. I love its large, pink, blousy flowers which stand up surprisingly well to rain. The flowers seem to be larger in its first flush, which can be really spectacular, and then they seem to reduce in size, continuing intermittently until flowering finishes in late autumn. The growth is upright and rather lanky and needs careful training. It's not particularly scented, but is rather light and sweet. The foliage is exceptionally healthy and has acceptable disease-resistance. I have found that if it's grown in shade, the flowers hold their colour longer. This is a very tall-growing rose and, once established, you will need to use a ladder to reach the top when pruning.

Climbing Hybrid Tea | 1901
H: 5m x S: 2.5m

FRANÇOIS JURANVILLE

For me, this characterful rose always has a strong presence when in full bloom. The double flowers are a rich, deep, lobster-pink with darker lowlights. Exceptionally free-flowering, its foliage is dark green and the new growth is tinged bronze. This rose benefits from a large support if being trained against a wall. It's necessary to prune it on a regular basis when it's established, to prevent the top growth becoming too overcrowded and heavy. It can be prone to blackspot but don't let this put you off, as it can easily be treated. It's magnificent in full flower.

Wichuriana Rambler | 1906
H: 4.5m x S: 3m

MORNING JEWEL
(see page 109)

One of the best modern, pink-flowered climbing roses, with attractive rich pink flowers throughout the summer. The foliage is mid-green and glossy and has good disease-resistance. It should be lightly pruned when dormant and responds well to regular feeding. It may take a few seasons to settle in but, once it's fully established, you can expect spectacular displays each year.

Modern Climber | 1968
H: 4m x S: 2.5m

SOUVENIR DE GEORGES PERNET
(see page 41)

This is a climbing rose of great vigour. It's best grown against a sunny wall, where it can reach its full height. The flowers are large, full and a rich pink. The scent is light. It has good disease-resistance and enjoys rich, deep soil. It's a super rose which gives a great flush in June, followed by occasional flowers afterwards. Unfortunately, it's not widely available.

Climbing Rose
H: 3m x S: 4m

deep pink/cerise

ALOHA

'Aloha' is regarded as one of the great climbing roses. Its strong, fruity, sweetly scented flowers are Hybrid Tea in shape, with attractively pointed buds. They are a deep rose-pink with overtones of salmon, dark pink and even terracotta. The petals are darker on the reverse, which gives the rose a two-toned look. It repeat-flowers and responds well to a warm, sunny position, but also suits a rainy climate. For best results, give it rich soil. You can grow it either as a  climber or as a large freestanding Shrub. With careful training, it even makes an excellent pillar rose. It's an ideal rose for cutting, as the flowers hold very well in water.

Modern Climber | 1949
H: 3m x S: 2m

AMERICAN PILLAR
(see page 78)

'American Pillar' is a vigorous and strongly growing Rambling rose that produces a profusion of single flowers in clusters. They are deep pink in colour with a white central eye. The flowers gradually fade to a paler shade before the petals fall. The rich green foliage is large and susceptible to mildew. Some pruning should be carried out after flowering. This rose needs an open, sunny spot and benefits from the application of a mulch to help keep moisture in the soil during summer.

Wichuriana Rambler | 1902
H: 6m x W: 4.5m

SUPER DOROTHY
(syn. 'Hedloro')

This improvement on the famous rose 'Dorothy Perkins' has the advantage of being resistant to mildew and of repeat-flowering well, though it's not as strong-  growing. The flowers are a darker shade than those of 'Dorothy Perkins'. They are deep pink with a white patch in the centre and grow in large panicles of between twenty and forty. It comes into flower late, only finishing with the first frosts. It makes an excellent weeping standard.

Wichuriana Rambler | 1986
H: 3m x S: 2m

ZÉPHIRINE DROUHIN
(see page 47)

This is a thornless climber, which makes it ideal for archways. The flowers are a bright, rich pink and open to a beautiful loose, informal shape. The scent is sweet and heady. It grows well against a wall but also can be grown as a bush. It has produced two sports worth looking for: 'Kathleen Harrop' (rose-pink) and 'Martha' (pale pink with fuller flowers). To really get the best from this rose, it's necessary to plant it in good-quality, free-draining soil. It will happily flower in sun or shade. It can suffer from blackspot and it will be necessary to keep an eye out for this. It's a rose that should be lightly pruned and, if grown as a climber, it will need regular feeding.

Bourbon Rose | 1868
H: 3m x S: 2m

striped & bi-coloured

HANDEL
(see page 31)

I find that Handel is slow to establish but given time, it makes an excellent climber. It flowers over a particularly long period and is noted for holding well in the rain. Handel can be prone to blackspot and mildew, so it's really important to keep a close eye on it, especially late in the season. It has the advantage of not producing too many thorns, which is a good thing if it's growing where people have to pass by at close quarters. In soils that are prone to drying out, this rose will really benefit from the use of a mulch, which will help to keep moisture in the soil while the plant is flowering. Do not prune this rose too hard; pruning is only really necessary for keeping a tidy shape and removing dead or crossed branches.

Modern Climber | 1965
H: 3m x S: 2m

PHYLLIS BIDE
(see page 61)

This is such a charming and unusual rambler. It grows loosely and repeat-flowers well. The flowers are a mix of orange, yellow, apricot and pink with a pleasant, soft fragrance. It requires only light pruning which helps to keep the plant tidy and prevents it from becoming too top heavy. It really responds to being grown in a sunny spot. It is generally disease-resistant and appreciates fertile, free-draining soil.

Polyantha | 1923
H: 3m x S: 2m

rose care

buying a rose

I always feel a great thrill when I go out to buy roses. For me it's not just retail therapy, it's the anticipation of what's to come. When I hold a rose plant in my hand, it may be nothing more than a bunch of twigs and a few roots – but I can see past that. I can imagine the rose growing in my garden and how it will transform a particular area. I can see the colour of its flowers and I can almost enjoy its scent.

It pays to do a little bit of homework in advance of buying a rose. You need to ask yourself several questions, starting with, 'Where do I want this rose for?' Many of us fall into the trap of buying a plant and not having the proper spot or place for it. We end up with what looks like an intensive-care unit on the side of our patio – loads of plants all sitting in pots, all those impulse buys, and all without a proper home. So having the position already worked out for the rose you're buying is the first step. The next major consideration is soil quality. If your chosen planting spot has poor-quality soil, it will really pay to do some work on it beforehand.

Selecting the right quality

I'm a great believer in the saying 'You get what you pay for' and the same applies to buying a rose. If you buy bargain offers, you can end up with poor and inferior plants, so be cautious. That rose might look really good in a flyer that comes with a gardening magazine, but when it arrives, you may be disappointed with its size and quality. It really is worthwhile to invest some money in top-quality plants. You need to go to a reputable grower or a reliable garden centre who offer quality stock that they're prepared to stand over. This will ensure that you're getting the variety that's true to name and that you're also getting a plant that has been grown to point of sale by a professional nurseryman.

If you're really keen to buy quality, hard-to-find roses, I recommend you approach some specialist rose nurseries. These are growers whose nurseries are devoted to nothing but growing and selling roses and their reputations are based on the quality of what they produce. Otherwise, for buying roses in general, I recommend going to a quality garden centre where you can seek the advice of professional staff.

Bare-rooted roses

Traditionally, roses were sold as bare-rooted plants. This means that they were lifted from the ground while dormant in winter, their roots were wrapped and protected from drying out, and they were sold for immediate planting, provided weather conditions were suitable. Bare-rooted roses are still sold and are available from garden centres today. Many of the specialist rose nurseries, including mail-order nurseries, sell their roses

this way, too. You can buy bare-rooted plants any time during the dormant season, usually from when the first frost hits the plants until early March, before they start back into regrowth.

When you buy a bare-rooted rose, it has usually been cut back sufficiently so that there is no need for pruning, except if you find some dead or broken growth. When you're selecting a bare-rooted rose, make sure that the root system hasn't been allowed to dehydrate. You're looking for a rose that has been freshly lifted, with its roots well-wrapped to protect them from drying out. Also check that the roses are clearly labelled and that the stems look fresh and healthy. Avoid those with damage and, if possible,

avoid any with die-back, where the tops of the stems are turning brown.

Pre-packed roses

Pre-packed roses are usually bare-rooted roses sold in supermarkets and hardware-store chains. They have the advantage of being inexpensive, but a word of caution is needed. If these roses are left in the packs too long, they may start into growth too early and you may end up with long, straggly growth within the bag. This is to be avoided at all costs. Also, depending on where they've been stored, pre-packed roses are prone to drying out, and they'll die before they ever get a chance at growth. So just be careful and make sure that you examine the rose carefully before purchasing. You can get some good buys, but you can also have some disasters.

Container-grown roses

Container-grown roses are plants that are established in pots. They are available for planting all year round, but you should avoid planting when the ground is frozen, if the soil is too wet, or if it's too dry. They can even be planted when they are in full flower, which allows the gardener a longer period for planting and gives you the advantage of being able to select a healthy rose which you can see in flower. Container-grown roses are always a little bit more expensive, as you are paying for an established plant. The advantage of planting a container-grown rose is that it settles in quickly and gets off to a great start.

Selecting a healthy rose

When buying a rose, look for a plant with a minimum of two or three strong, healthy stems. I put more emphasis on having good, healthy stems than on the quantity of stems. These stems should ideally be green and fresh-looking with no sign of wrinkles. In the dormant period, the buds should just about be visible.

Have a look at these to make sure they look fresh, too.

If you are buying container-grown plants, look for really good, healthy foliage. Avoid any roses that have signs of disease, as well as any with yellowing leaves. The foliage should be bright and clean. I also recommend that you check that container-grown roses are not pot-bound. This indicates that they have been growing in the pot for too long and the roots have become compacted. It's easy to check for this by gently tipping the rose out of the container. However, if

you're doing this early in the year I recommend caution because the rose may not yet have become established in its pot. You'll end up with compost everywhere and a rather embarrassed look on your face! Ideally, what you're looking for is a well-developed root system. The roots should look healthy and white and not overcrowded.

If you have any questions when you are buying, don't be afraid to ask a member of staff for advice. Good garden centres are always happy to help.

HEELING IN

If you have purchased bare-rooted roses from a mail-order nursery or collected them from a garden centre, and you're not ready to plant, it's essential that you don't let the root system dry out. What you must do is 'heel' them in.
1. In a sheltered spot of the garden, dig a small trench and place the plant in this.

2. Heel in by using soil from the trench to cover the root system and graft union or budding point (this is the swollen area between the roots and branches.)
3. Cover the budding point with about five centimetres of soil. Gently firm the soil in around the roots so that it is making contact with them but is not compacted.

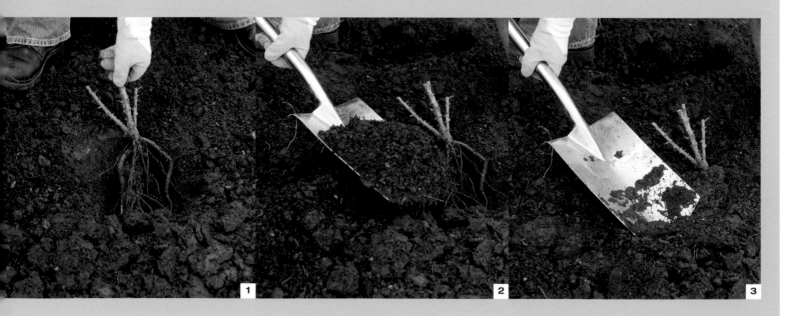

planting a rose

When planting a rose, you will have a choice; depending on the time of year, you'll either be faced with a bare-rooted rose or a container-grown rose (see page 169). Whichever one you plant, the final results will be the same, although the planting methods differ.

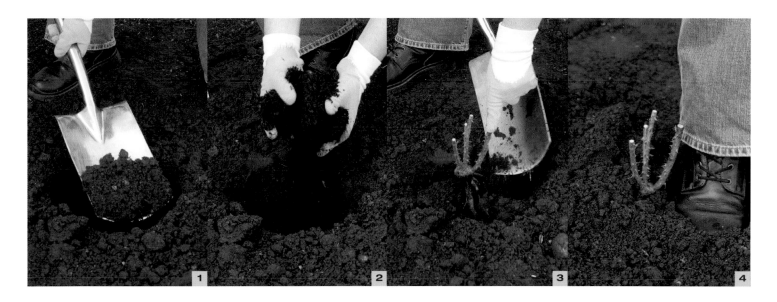

Planting a bare-rooted rose

Bare-rooted roses should come wrapped to protect the roots from drying out. If you're unable to plant them immediately, it's a good idea to heel them in as a temporary measure (see left). Bare-rooted roses are traditionally planted in autumn and into winter. Providing that weather conditions are good and that the soil is manageable, it's a very straight-forward procedure. Before you plant a rose, identify the graft union or budding point. This swollen area between the roots and the branches is the spot where the rose was originally grafted.

1. The planting hole should be deep enough to cover the union so that it is approximately two centimetres below soil level. This helps to deter suckers. You should also make the hole wider than the rose's spread-out roots to help the rose's stability as it matures.

2. Once the hole is dug, you need to break up the soil in the bottom, which helps the roots to penetrate deeper into the soil. I usually do this job with a fork. At this point, I often sprinkle in a little home-made, well-rotted garden compost. I also mix some compost into the soil that I've removed from the planting hole so that's ready to use to fill back in around the root system.

3. The next thing is to position the rose in the planting hole, spreading out the roots, while keeping the plant upright. I add some soil into the bottom of the hole as I fill in around the roots, which helps to support the rose. At this stage, I gently shake the plant so that soil trickles in between the tangle of roots, helping to avoid air pockets.

4. Gradually fill up the planting hole, gently firming the soil with your feet. It's important to firm the rose well into position, as winter weather can easily rock and destabilise newly planted roses. Once the new roots start to grow in the spring, your plant will require regular watering.

Planting a container-grown rose

Container-grown roses can be planted at any time of year, weather permitting. It's essential that the compost in the container is thoroughly moistened before you plant. Never depend on rain. Instead, I usually soak container-grown roses the night before in a bucketful of water. I sometimes stand the roses in their containers in a wheelbarrow full of water if I'm planting several at one time. You've then got the wheelbarrow handy for transporting them to the planting spot.

1. Make the planting hole generous. It should be wider than the pot and deep enough to cover the union. It's common in container-grown roses to find the union above soil level. When you plant, though, it's important to plant deeper so that the union is completely covered by approximately two centimetres of soil. It's a good idea to check the depth and width of the planting hole while the rose is still in the pot, so that you are confident that it fits perfectly into its new

position. Prepare the planting hole by breaking up the soil in the bottom lightly with a fork. Have some home-made garden compost or well-rotted organic matter to hand, to be incorporated into the soil.

2. Ensuring that the rose has been well watered in advance, it's time to remove it from its pot. Do this gently to avoid breaking the young, fibrous roots. Never grasp the base of the rose and pull, as this can disturb the roots. Instead, wearing a glove to protect your hand from thorns, turn the pot upside down, and gently tap the edge of the pot to free the root ball. If it's slow to separate, you may need to gently squeeze the sides of the pot.

3. If a rose has become fully established in the container, it will be necessary to tease out roots at the base of the root ball to encourage them to travel into your garden soil.

4. Once the pot comes free, gently place the root ball into the planting hole in its final position. Carefully and gradually add soil and compost

or organic matter to fill the gap between the planting hole and the root ball. Firm the soil in gently as you go, using your feet. Once planted, water well. I believe that nine out of ten newly planted roses that die do so as a result of drought, so water generously, whatever the weather. The newly planted rose will require regular watering for six to eight months while it establishes its new root system into the soil.

TIP

If your roses are grown in polythene pots, it's possible to remove the pot gently using a sharp knife while they are sitting in the planting hole. It's more difficult, though, to remove a rigid plastic pot in this way. Care should be taken, as the root ball can be very heavy, especially when moist. The weight of the compost can make it pull away from the roots, causing damage, so remove the pot as close as possible to the planting hole so that you are not carrying it any distance.

watering and feeding

To get the very best out of your roses, you will need to feed them. So unless you are prepared to do that, you really should forget about growing them altogether. In poor soils, unless the rose is particularly suited to those conditions, you will find that growth is weak and flowering is not at its best.

Roses are demanding plants because, when you think about it, it takes a lot of energy to produce such spectacular blooms. The older antique rose varieties, in particular, are a little like prima donnas who like to choose their food from the à la carte menu. I have seen this time and time again in my own garden. They are what I call 'greedy' roses.

Put simply, I find that if you treat your roses well, they will reward you. No matter what type of rose, if you practise good cultivation techniques, are prepared to give them the feed they need and water them when necessary, you are guaranteed the kind of display that makes the whole process of gardening and growing these wonderful flowers worthwhile.

Soil considerations

I always recommend that anyone who enjoys gardening gets to know their soil. It's the foundation of all growth and, by having some understanding of it, you will have greater insight into

cultivation. Roses like a slightly acid soil. They're happy with a neutral to acid pH (pH5–7). You can easily find your soil pH by buying an inexpensive kit, available from most hardware outlets and garden centres. If your soil is very alkaline, you can add sulphur chips at approximately 25g per square metre, which will help move the pH towards neutral and acid. It's always important to follow the instructions, so that you don't add too much.

The next thing with soil is to make sure that it is free-draining, as roses resent having their roots sitting in water. If your soil becomes waterlogged, you will have to provide drainage to deal with the problem. It may be necessary to get professional advice if the site is exceptionally badly drained, otherwise it can be sufficient to add extra grit to the soil to carry surface moisture away from the root system. At all costs, roots should not be sitting in water for any length of time.

Once these matters have been attended to, we can all improve the quality and texture of our soil, and its fertility, by adding organic matter. This can be in the form of well-rotted farmyard manure or home-made garden compost. As well as improving the soil's texture and fertility, it will also help with drainage. If you experiment, you'll quickly see the difference between a rose bush grown in soil that is rich in organic matter

versus one grown in soil that is poor in organic matter. The results are always clearly visible.

Different types of feed

ORGANIC FEEDS

Using organic feeds is the best way of improving the condition of your soil and making your own compost is a great way of starting. It means that you are recycling your vegetable waste and helping to maintain soil fertility at the same time. Remember that the compost you make is a feed and should be mixed with your soil. It makes a fantastic addition when you're planting new roses. It can also be used as a mulch spread around your plants on the surface of the soil, from where its nutrients will slowly work their way down to the roots.

If you're using manure, I always recommend wearing gloves as, for hygiene reasons, you shouldn't handle it. The manure should always be well rotted. If it isn't, the acids in the decomposing manure can scorch or burn the roots of your plants. The manure could come from several sources. Garden centres now offer farmyard manure pre-packed in bags or, if you live in the country, you may be able to get stable bedding from a local farm. Like garden compost, manure is a feed and you should never grow a rose in anything else but this.

It should be mixed through the soil or used as a mulch spread on the surface of the soil around the plant. To my mind, home-made garden compost and well-rotted farmyard manure are worth their weight in gold. They are the difference between transforming a plant from ordinary into top quality.

FERTILISERS AND LIQUID FEEDS

There are many proprietary chemical fertilisers available. These are easy to use and are ideal for feeding at the beginning of the growing season. Be sure to follow the instructions and, in general, it's better to give less rather than more. It's not like cooking, where you might add an extra dash of this or an extra pinch of that.

I recommend a light sprinkling of a general commercial granular rose feed around the roses in late spring, just as their new growth is developing. I do this again after the first flush of flowers to encourage repeat-flowering roses to bring on another flush. Don't allow the granular fertiliser to come in direct contact with the plant but, instead, sprinkle it lightly around the plant on the soil surface. Because of its chemical nature, neat granular fertiliser can scorch foliage.

You also have the option of using a slow-release granular feed. This feeds the plant slowly throughout the growing season, as and when the plant needs the nutrients. My greediest roses usually get a light sprinkling to ensure they're being fussed over.

Then there are liquid feeds. There are lots of different brands available and, as with the granular feeds, always follow the instructions carefully. Never use a liquid feed on a dry plant, as dry roots are more vulnerable to being damaged by the chemical composition of the feed; the soil should be evenly moist or barely damp before you apply the feed. Do this early in the morning or late in the evening and avoid splashing the foliage. Liquid feeds are particularly valuable for roses grown in containers or large pots. I recommend little and often for established roses.

Finally, there is foliar feed. This is a soluble solution which is sprayed onto both sides of the foliage – a job which should be done out of direct sunlight to prevent the magnifying effect of the sun's rays through the droplets, which can cause burning of the leaves. Nutrients are absorbed immediately into the plant, like a tonic. A foliar feed is very beneficial for plants that are under stress and is especially useful if you notice that your roses are suffering from nutrient deficiency. If in doubt, take a leaf to a local garden centre or qualified horticulturalist who can examine it and advise you.

Watering in summer

The key to your plants getting the nutrients they need is, of course, water, as it carries the nutrients to the cells of the plant. Roses benefit from plenty of water in summer, but aim for a

happy medium – you don't want the soil too dry, or too wet, as roses don't appreciate sitting in water. If your soil is sandy and very free-draining, it's a good idea to soak your roses two or three times a week in high summer.

CAUTION

I stress caution with any of the feeding I have mentioned. Please, please, don't overdo it. Giving a small amount of feed on a regular basis is much better than giving a lot every now and then.

If you have your roses growing in pots, try to keep the soil or compost evenly moist.

Weeding and mulching

Keeping roses weed-free is essential, since weeds create competition, robbing the roses of the nutrients they desperately need. One way of preventing weeds is to use a mulch. Not only will it help to keep the soil cool and the moisture in, but it will also seal in weed seeds, and so prevent the weeds from germinating. There are lots of different commercial mulches available. Be careful of mushroom compost, as it is very alkaline and may change the pH of your soil. I recommend home-made garden compost, well-rotted manure, leaf mould, cocoa shell and chipped bark. I have even used spent hops with great success. Check out what's available locally and have a go.

pruning and training

Pruning

The reason we prune roses is to encourage fresh new growth which will carry healthy, strong flowers for the coming season. We also prune to remove dead or diseased growth and to improve the shape of the plant. If you never prune, the rose will still grow and flower but may not look as tidy and may not produce as many flowers. Before pruning any rose, it needs to be established and to have had at least twelve months of growth so that a basic structure is in place which is strong enough to be cut back.

Tools

I recommend that you go out and buy the best-quality secateurs that you can afford. They are essential for doing a good job. They can be expensive but it's money well spent and will make an enormous difference to the quality of your results. It's also a good idea to have pruning loppers – again, buy good quality – and if you have large roses, particularly shrub roses, a

FROM LEFT: Saw, loppers and secateurs

pruning saw is invaluable for getting rid of extra-thick branches. Always clean secateurs, loppers and pruning saws after you have used them. This helps to avoid spreading disease. You will also need a good-quality pair of gardening gloves; buy a pair that is strong enough to withstand rose thorns.

Technique

When you are pruning roses, you need to cut above a bud. This is best done when the buds are beginning to develop and are showing quite clearly

on the plant. The ideal cut is approximately 30mm above the bud and should slope gently away from the bud. This slope is designed to carry moisture away from the bud. Never cut down behind or below the bud as this can cause the stem to die back at this point, which would kill off the new bud. Sometimes, buds may remain dormant on the plant and be difficult to see. If this is the case, look for a leaf scar – the place where a leaf once joined the stem – and just above this is where a dormant bud lies.

When pruning, select an outward-facing bud to make your cut. This encourages a good shape to your rose. If you are pruning climbing roses or

Always use clean secateurs for pruning

ramblers, you must look for buds that point in the direction of the wall or support, rather than buds that point outwards, away from the support. If you prune above these, the new growth will grow outwards too, creating a system of stems that is far more difficult to train.

BUSH ROSES

With bush roses, the first thing I do is to remove any dead wood and take out any stems that may be crossing or rubbing against each other. When I was first taught how to prune a rose, I was always told to also remove any

WHEN TO PRUNE

In Ireland, we traditionally pruned our roses by 17 March, St. Patrick's Day. This was used as a rough guide to get the job done. Our winters, though, have become milder so Irish gardeners are now pruning earlier with no harm or ill effects to our plants. In fact, there is no exact time by which you have to have your roses pruned, providing that the job is done while the plants are dormant.

In October, I lightly cut back the tops of my roses to take off any heavy or excessive weight. This reduces the chances of the wind rocking the bushes through winter, which may cause damage to the base of the plant. However, it's not really a proper pruning.

Then I usually prune my old roses just after Christmas, saving this job for a mild January day (if such a thing exists!)

Bush pruning

stems that were less than the thickness of a pencil, but now a new school of thought tells us that these smaller, twiggy branches are an important part of the plant's growing system. Though these stems on bush roses will not generally carry flowers, they do produce leaves which manufacture food for the plant. So I have now stopped removing the smaller, twiggy

TIP

Floribundas generally have lighter stems, so I only cut back to about one-third of their length. The same applies to Miniature roses.

branches, unless there is a need to. After checking over the bush for dead and crossing growth, I then start the complete prune, cutting back stems to approximately 20cm above the ground. This encourages strong shoots which will carry good flowers.

SHRUB ROSES

Many shrub roses grow to a considerable size, so you need to stand back from the bush and assess the job before you start. First, remove dead stems and tidy up any branches that are crossing.

An established shrub rose has main branches that are responsible for carrying the flowering framework. If necessary, for example if they are overcrowding the plant or if they have become very old, some of these main branches can be removed or reduced in length. Keep in mind that you want to leave a well-shaped bush. You can then cut back the secondary framework of branches, which grow from these main stems, leaving at most four or five buds on these secondary stems. These will then produce flowering growth for the coming season.

CLIMBING AND RAMBLING ROSES

It takes two or three years for a climbing or rambling rose to become established. There is no need for pruning while they are settling in. Your main priority in these early stages is to train the new growths in the direction you want them to grow, supporting the climbing or rambling stems as needed. While the new framework is developing, spread the branches by tying them in to trellis or other supports.

After the third year of growth, you can prune your climbing and rambling roses. The first task is to remove any dead wood. Secondly, any weak branches can be tidied back to the first bud from the main stem. This will encourage new, strong growth.

Then, to encourage flowering, I recommend you cut all side shoots back to half their length. Rambling roses require less pruning than climbing roses. I suggest that with ramblers, you spend more time on tidying the plant than cutting back hard. It's a case of keeping the ramblers under control and preventing them from becoming too top heavy.

The same applies to ground-cover roses. It's more a case of tidying up rather than a hard cutting back.

Training

Spread the branches of your climbing rose out over the support to achieve an even coverage of it. By arching the branches, you are encouraging more flowering shoots to develop, so training climbers and ramblers in this way will ensure a better crop of flowers. You can help things along by keeping the shape of the plant in your mind and selecting outward-facing buds when you are making your pruning cuts. This helps avoid ending up with a tangled centre.

If you are training roses over archways or pergolas, make sure that these are strong and when you are tying branches in to the support, make sure that the ties are not too tight, as this may cause damage to stems. You should check ties every few months and loosen or replace them if they are becoming tight.

Climbing and rambling roses can even be trained along the top of a low wall.

propagation

One of the most satisfying and rewarding ways of increasing your rose stock is to grow your own from cuttings. Not only does this save you money but it also provides you with new, healthy, fresh stock to swap with neighbours and friends, which adds to your collection of roses. I remember taking cuttings (with permission, of course) of a variety growing in an old Irish garden. This allowed me to grow the rose myself and later gave me a chance to identify it, as the owner did not know the name.

Roses from seed

If you wish to raise a lot of roses, seed is one of the most economical ways of doing so and is ideal for producing species roses, rootstock or hedging. The seed will need a period of cold before it will germinate. A good way to achieve this is to chill the seed in the fridge for six weeks before bringing it back into the warmth of an average room for immediate sowing. Sowing seed directly outside can take two periods of chilling to break the dormancy before germination, so patience is needed.

It's essential to remove the seed from the rosehip before sowing, as the hips contain a germination inhibitor. When sowing seeds in pots or seed trays outside, it's also a good idea to protect the seed with wire mesh to deter mice and other rodents from eating the seeds in winter.

By planting into pots and trays and leaving them outside in the winter, you expose the seed to the cold and rain, which helps break down its dormancy. In spring, you can bring the pots or seed trays into an unheated greenhouse, where you will see your first seedlings emerge. This is always an exciting time.

1. Remove the seeds from the rosehips before you start. This can be done in autumn when the hips are fully coloured and ripe. The seeds are like small cream to brown pips.

2. Sow the seeds in a proprietary seed compost in a flowerpot, mixing in a little grit with this to guarantee good drainage. Position the seeds on top of the compost and cover lightly with horticultural grit. This helps to secure the seed and prevents the rain washing it away. Place the pot in a clear plastic bag, which acts as a mini-greenhouse, helping to maintain moisture and giving protection to both seeds and seedlings.

3. When seedlings appear and the first true leaves have developed – the leaves that follow the seed-leaf stage – pot them on into individual 8–10cm pots. Grow these on until they are large enough to transplant outside, that is when they are large enough to handle and when you feel they have developed a strong root system.

Taking cuttings is simpler than you might think. Though people are happy to grow plants from seed or to take geranium cuttings, they often hesitate when it comes to growing roses from cuttings, but they root very easily so I encourage you to have a go and grow your own. Just follow a few simple techniques.

There are two types of cuttings – semi-ripe wood cuttings and hardwood cuttings.

Taking hardwood cuttings

Roses can be grown from hardwood cuttings. It is usual for them to root easily. The resulting plants will have their own root systems and you won't have any problems with suckers.

Hardwood cuttings are taken outdoors in autumn or early winter and must be inserted in light, well-drained soil in a sheltered spot. You should choose ripe wood, ideally, selected from strong side shoots with a woody base, as these will not rot. The best cuttings have dormant buds

Taking softwood cuttings

near the base; these are rich in auxins, the hormones that produce new roots. You might also choose to use a hormone-rooting powder or liquid. These are widely available and are particularly useful if you are rooting difficult varieties, as they encourage them to root faster.

1. Take cuttings in autumn when weather conditions are still warm and there is moisture in the soil. It can even be done in early winter. Select rose stems that were produced during the year, as these will be well ripened by now and therefore are ideal for hardwood cuttings.

2. It's important to make sure that each cutting has at least four nodes. If at all possible – though this may not be the case later in the winter – keep a few leaves at the top of each cutting as these help to increase the success rate of rooting.

3. Prepare the soil in advance by digging it over so that it's easy to insert the cuttings. Insert the cuttings into the soil, firming each one into position with your fingers. This is important, as you want to avoid the cuttings rocking in the wind. Water in well.

4. Cuttings will take up to a year to root and establish. You can then move them on to their final flowering position in the autumn/winter of the following year. With less vigorous varieties, it is a good idea to leave the cuttings in for an extra twelve-month period to allow them to develop a strong root system.

Taking softwood cuttings

The best time to take softwood cuttings is early in the year, ideally just after your roses have finished their first flush of flowers. Select a cutting with several closely spaced buds near its base. These will develop growth from beneath the surface of the soil, helping to produce a strong, well-balanced, shapely bush. Trim off the leaves lower down the cutting but always include a few leaves on the top, as these will provide energy for the new cutting. You will need to place these cuttings either in a cold frame or in a pot covered with a clear plastic bag.

1. Select young growth and trim the cutting just below a leaf joint. This is where the roots will develop from. Always use a sharp knife or secateurs.

2. Cut off the softest growth at the top of the cutting, leaving a firm base and a pair of leaves at the top.

3. Dip the bottom of the cutting in hormone-rooting powder or liquid.

4. Position the cutting in well-drained compost in a cold frame or in a pot. Water.

5. If using a pot, cover with a clear plastic bag and place in a bright position away from direct sunlight, as this will damage the cutting. A north-facing windowsill or a cold frame out of direct sunlight is ideal.

pests and diseases

Gardeners are becoming more conscious about the chemicals that they use. Legislation has demanded the removal of many pesticides and fungicides from the market. So to behave responsibly, we now need to explore how to deal with pests and diseases in an organic way. The problem is a special one in the case of roses, which can be high-maintenance.

Some gardeners I know have made a conscious decision not to grow rose varieties that are particularly prone to diseases like blackspot. Instead, they are opting for varieties that have proved to be resistant. This is one way of cutting back on the problem. Other gardeners have opted for purely organic methods. Then there are those who use organic methods with the intervention of garden chemicals if things get out of hand. So you have to decide what kind of gardener you're going to be before you tackle the pests and diseases that can make an impact on your roses.

I do my best to work with nature, trying to create a balance in my garden and encouraging nature's predators. However, every gardener will have his or her own views and, at the end of the day, it's up to you to decide how you're going to deal with insect pests and fungal diseases.

Pests

GREENFLY
Aphids, otherwise known as greenfly, are probably the biggest pest on roses. They do most damage when they congregate around young growth early in the season, sucking on the plant's sap, stunting the growing tip and distorting the developing foliage. Greenfly can be found around the new shoots and on the undersides of leaves. In my own garden, I find them most prevalent in late spring, but by encouraging natural insect predators, such as ladybirds, lacewings and hoverflies, I usually achieve a balance.

I find that using a high-pressure spray of water from a hose, dislodges them easily and helps to keep them in check. If you wish to use one of the many organic insecticides on the market, it's important to ensure that the spray comes in contact with the insect. On the chemical side, there are some very effective systemic insecticides. These should be used with great care. Always follow the instructions and avoid inhaling them.

Greenfly

Also, avoid using any spray in bright sunlight, as this may damage or scorch young foliage. Some gardeners plant garlic or marigolds near their roses to discourage pests, but I haven't found these to be effective myself.

CATERPILLARS
Caterpillars never become a major problem on roses, as they never seem to be present in sufficient quantities to do severe damage. I find, from time to time, that I have what I call a 'rogue' caterpillar, one that hides under leaves during the day, emerging in the evening to take chunks out of foliage or devour petals on flowers, leaving behind unsightly marks and damaged leaves. If you can find these by hunting them out carefully, they can easily be removed by hand. I have never found them such a nuisance that I had to resort to using a spray. I much prefer to leave them to the birds in my garden or to the wasps. It's great fun to watch a family of bluetits scour the rose garden for insects, dancing from one bush to another, picking away at their finds. This always gives me great pleasure. It's a double bonus – my roses get cleaned of pests and I have the fun of watching the beauty of the birds.

FROM LEFT: Blackspot, rust and powdery mildew

RED SPIDER MITE

Red spider mites can be a problem, especially in dry climates. They hate moisture, so this is the key to dealing with them. A light misting of water, out of direct sunlight, will discourage them. If you have a really bad infestation, where you will find the finest net-like web on the growing tips of your roses and the foliage turning yellow, you need to deal with it by using an appropriate insecticide. Red spider mite can also be a problem in greenhouses or conservatories where climbing roses are grown. Increasing the humidity helps to discourage them.

Diseases

BLACKSPOT AND RUST

Blackspot and rust are a common fungal problem on roses. Blackspot is more prevalent and appears as spots or black patches on the leaves. The leaves eventually turn yellow and, if the infestation is bad, the leaves will start to drop off. If the problem isn't that bad, remove the leaves by hand and burn them. Avoid adding them to your compost heap. Some rose varieties are more susceptible than others, but good cultivation can help them to withstand an attack. When plants are hungry they are more vulnerable, so good feeding is a start. If you have to resort to a fungicide, be it organic or chemical, you may need to use it on a fortnightly basis, starting in May until the end of September. Hygiene is very important too, and the removal of fallen leaves is crucial to controlling this problem. Otherwise the spores can remain dormant in the soil to be splashed up by rain onto the leaves again next year, and then the whole cycle starts all over. Mulching can also help control blackspot, as it seals in any spores that may have lodged on the soil. This same treatment applies to rust, which manifests itself as orange or rust-coloured pustules on the backs of leaves. The pustules eventually turn black. Rust is usually seen in July.

POWDERY MILDEW

Powdery mildew is easy to control if caught early. The symptoms are a white, powdery coating that appears on the foliage and flower buds. If left unchecked, the leaves will become distorted, will pale in colour, and eventually fall. Depending on weather conditions, powdery mildew can spread rapidly. In bad cases, plants can be weakened, so much so that it will stop the plant flowering. You will need to spray with a fungicide.

Again, good cultivation helps to strengthen the plant, creating some natural resistance. Any diseased foliage should always be burned rather than composted. These fungal diseases often occur when the weather is hot and humid, for it is at such times that plants are most susceptible as they are under stress.

RIGHT: Encourage bluetits to visit the garden. They'll make short work of harmful caterpillars.

glossary

ALBA ROSE
A cross between *R. damascena* and *R. canina,* Alba roses have distinctive and very attractive grey-green foliage and flower in early summer in shades from white to pink.

BALLING
When flower buds fail to open, usually because the petals become wet and stick together. A wet-weather problem.

BARE-ROOTED ROSE
A rose dug up from the ground and sold without being potted up.

BOURBON ROSE
The first repeat-flowering roses developed from the Hybrid China roses. They derive their name from the location of the first members of the class, the Île de Bourbon in the Indian Ocean. Plant size ranges from 500cm to 4.5m. Repeat-blooming.

BUD UNION
This is the point where the bud and rootstock are joined.

BUDDING
The grafting of a bud into the neck of a rootstock. A propagation method used in commercial rose production.

BUTTON EYE
This is where petals are folded inwards to form a button in the centre of the bloom. It is a characteristic of some old-fashioned varieties.

CENTIFOLIA ROSE
These Dutch hybridised roses derive their class name from the fact the flowers often contain more than 100 petals. Plants are 1–2.5m tall and winter-hardy. Once-blooming.

CHINA ROSE
These roses first appeared in the mid-eighteenth century and their long flowering season encouraged breeders to use them. There are bush and climbing forms.

CLIMBING SPORT
A climbing mutation of a Bush rose that produces longer stems but has identical flowers to the Bush.

DAMASK ROSE
Best known for their intense heavy fragrance, Damask roses generally range in size from 1m to 2m. Some varieties are repeat-blooming.

DIE-BACK
A progressive dying back of the stems from the tips.

DORMANT BUD
A bud which has not yet started into growth.

ENGLISH ROSE
The name given to the group of roses bred by David Austin, combining the qualities of old and modern roses.

FLORIBUNDA ROSE
Bears flowers in clusters or trusses. The form of the flower is usually lighter than that of the Hybrid Tea.

GALLICA ROSE
Some of the oldest of all cultivated roses, making compact plants. Once-blooming.

GRAFTING
The joining of a stem or bud of one plant onto the stem of another.

GRAFT UNION
See BUD UNION

HEELING IN
The temporary planting of new roses that are awaiting better weather conditions to allow proper planting.

HYBRID MUSK ROSE
Emerged early in the twentieth century. Flowers are produced in clusters and are usually scented.

HYBRID PERPETUAL ROSE
Characterised by their repeat bloom, plant size (about 2m tall, upright), fragrance and colour range (mostly pinks and reds), Hybrid Perpetuals superseded the Bourbons in the nineteenth century.

HYBRID TEA ROSE
Hybrid Tea roses feature high-centred, long-stemmed flowers (usually one per

stem), and bloom on upright, narrow plants in six-week flushes.

LEAF SCAR
The mark left where a leaf originally joined the stem.

MOSS ROSE
Named for the mossy thorn growth on the flower stalk, just below the bloom and sepals. This group of roses releases a naturally occurring mixture of oil and resin – often pine-scented – when the moss is rubbed between the fingers.

MULCH
A layer of organic matter placed around rose bushes to conserve moisture in the soil, prevent the germination of weed seed and to contribute nutrients to the plant.

NOISETTE ROSE
Noisette roses are large and sprawling, often reaching up to 6m tall. Blooms are produced in fragrant clusters.

OLD ROSE
A general term for old-fashioned roses.

PANICLE
A branched cluster of flowers.

POLYANTHA ROSE
Characterised by a profusion of flowers in many colours and a tidy growth habit, it was Polyanthas that were combined with Hybrid Teas to create the Floribundas.

PORTLAND ROSE
This small group of roses was derived from crosses involving Hybrid Gallica, Damask, Centifolia and Hybrid China. Named in honour of the Duchess of Portland.

QUARTERED
This is a term often used to describe the unfolding shape of certain roses, which appear to have four segments or quarters to the unfolding bloom.

RAMBLER/
RAMBLING ROSE
This describes a growth habit which is rambling and free-growing rather than upright, as happens with a climbing rose.

RECURVED
Refers to curling petals, and in the case of roses it usually means that the petals are curving outwards.

ROOT BALL
The collective root system which is exposed before planting.

ROOTSTOCK
This is the host root system of the plant onto which the selected cultivated variety will be budded.

ROSEHIP/HIP
The fruit of a rose, which can often be decorative on some varieties.

RUGOSA ROSE
A group of tough roses, dense and robust in form with thorny stems and thick, heavily veined leaves.

SCION
The term given to the bud which is used for grafting onto the rootstock.

SEMPERVIRENS ROSE
A group of rambling roses which usually hold their foliage, except in very cold winters.

SHRUB ROSE
This includes Modern Shrub roses. Shrub roses are easily characterised by their sprawling habit.

SPORT
A plant that shows mutation from its original parent.

SUCKER
A shoot that appears from below ground, growing directly from the rootstock.

TEA ROSE
Any of several cultivated roses derived from *Rosa odorata*, which is native to China. They have fragrant yellowish or pink flowers.

TRUSS
A number of flowers on one rose stem.

WICHURIANA ROSE
Descendents of *Rosa wichuriana*, which are noted for their healthy, dark green, glossy foliage.

resources

INTERNATIONAL ROSE GARDENS OPEN TO THE PUBLIC

Please check opening times in advance of travelling to any of these gardens.

AUSTRALIA
National Botanic Gardens
GPO Box 1777
Canberra
ACT 2601
Tel: + 61 (02) 6250 9450
www.anbg.gov.au

CANADA
Jardin Botanique de Montréal
4101 Sherbrooke St. E.,
Montréal
Quebec H1X 2B2
Tel: + 1 514 872 1400

Royal Botanical Gardens
680 Plains Road West
Hamilton/Burlington
Ontario L7T 4H4
Tel: + 1 905 527 1158
www.rbg.ca

DENMARK
Rosenplanteskolen I Løve
Plantevej 3
DK-4270 Høng
Tel: + 45 5886 9313
www.roses.dk

FRANCE
Les Chemins de la Rose
Parc de Courcilpleu
Route de Cholet
F-49 700 Doué la Fontaine
Tel: + 33 (0) 2 41 59 95 95
www.cheminsdelarose.fr

Le Jardin des Rosiers
86260 La Puye
Tel: + 33 (0) 5 49 46 99 96

Hôtel Baudy
Musée-Restaurant
81 rue Claude Monet
27620 Giverny
Tel: + 33 (0) 2 32 21 10 03

Roseraie de Berty
07110 Largentière
France
Tel: + 33 (0) 4 75 88 30 56
www.roseraie-de-berty.fr.st

Roseraie du Val-de-Marne
8, rue Albert Watel
94240 l'Haÿ-les-Roses
Tel: + 33 (0)1 43 99 82 80

GERMANY
Rosarium Sangerhausen
Steinberger Weg 3
D-06526 Sangerhausen
www.sangerhausen.de

IRELAND
Graigueconna
Old Connaught
Bray
Co. Wicklow
Tel: + 353 (0) 1 282 2273

National Botanic Gardens
Glasnevin
Dublin 9
Tel: + 353 (0)1 804 0300
www.botanicgardens.ie

St. Anne's Park & Rose Garden
Raheny
Dublin 5
Tel: + 353 (0) 1833 1859

Sir Thomas & Lady Dixon Park & City of Belfast International Rose Garden
Upper Malone Road
Belfast BT17 9LA
www.belfastcity.gov.uk

Tralee Rose Garden
Tralee Town Park
Tralee, Co. Kerry
www.tralee.ie

ITALY
La Giardini della Landriana
Via Campo di Carne 51
00040 Torre San Lorenzo
Ardea
Tel: + 39 (0) 6910 14140
www.giardinidellalandriana.it

NEW ZEALAND
Nancy Steen Rose Garden
Gladstone Road
Parnell
Auckland
Tel: + 64 (0) 9302 1252

UNITED KINGDOM
David Austin Rose Garden
Bowling Green Lane
Albrighton
Wolverhampton WV7 3HB
Tel: + 44 (01902) 376376
www.davidaustinroses.com

Kiftsgate
Chipping Campden
Gloucestershire GL55 6LN
Tel: + 44 (0)1386 438 777
www.kiftsgate.co.uk

Mottisfont Abbey Garden
nr. Romsey
Hampshire SO51 0LP
Tel: + 44 (0)1794 340 757

Peter Beales Rose Garden
London Road
Attleborough
Norfolk NR17 1AY
Tel: + 44 (0)1953 454 707
www.classicroses.co.uk

Royal Botanic Gardens, Kew
Richmond
Surrey TW9 3AB
Tel: + 44 (0)208 940 1171
www.rbgkew.org.uk

Royal National Rose Society
Chiswell Green Lane
Saint Albans
Hertfordshire AL2 3NR
Tel: + 44 (0)1727 850 461
www. rnrs.org

Sissinghurst Castle
Sissinghurst
Cranbrook
Kent TN17 2AB
Tel: + 44 (0)1580 710701

Sudeley Castle
Winchcombe
Cheltenham
Gloucestershire GL54 5JD
Tel: + 44 (0)1242 602 308
www.sudeleycastle.co.uk

Queen Mary's Rose Gardens
Regent's Park, London NW1

UNITED STATES

Berkeley Rose Garden
1200 Euclid Avenue
Berkeley
CA 94708
Tel: + 1 (510) 644 6566

Clark Botanic Garden
193 I. U. Willets Road
Albertson
NY 11507
Tel: + 1 (516) 484 8600
www.clarkbotanic.org

Elizabeth Park Rose Garden
150 Walbridge Road
West Hartford
CT 06119
Tel: + 1 (860) 242 0017
www.elizabethpark.com

**Governor John
Langdon House**
143 Pleasant Street
Portsmouth, NH 03801
Tel: + 1 (603) 436 3205

**Hampton National
Historic Site**
535 Hampton Lane
Towson, MD 21286
Tel: + 1 (410) 823 1309

Heirloom Old Garden Roses
24062 NE Riverside Drive
St. Paul, Oregon 97137
Tel: +1 (503) 538 1576
www.heirloomroses.com

Heritage Rose Gardens
Tanglewood Farms
16831 Mitchel Creek Drive
Fort Bragg, CA 95437

**Jackson & Perkins,
Bear Creek Gardens**
1 Rose Lane
Medford, Oregon 97137
Tel: + 1 (800) 292 4769
www.jproses.com

Longue Vue Gardens
7 Bamboo Road
New Orleans
LA 70124-1065
Tel: + 1 (504) 488 5488
www.longuevue.com

Los Angeles Arboretum
301 North Baldwin Avenue,
Arcadia
CA 91007
Tel: + 1 (626) 821 4623
www.arboretum.org

National Herb Garden
U.S. National Arboretum
3501 New York Avenue
NE Washington DC 20002
Tel: + 1 (202) 245 2726
www.usna.usda.gov

New York Botanical Garden
200th Street
Bronx
New York
NY 10458
Tel: + 1 (718) 817 8700
www.nybg.org

**Washington National
Cathedral Gardens**
Wisconsin Avenue NW
Washington DC 20016
Tel: + 1 (202) 537 2937

INTERNATIONAL ROSE SOCIETIES AND ORGANISATIONS

American Rose Society
P.O. Box 30,000
Shreveport
LA 71130-0030
Tel: +1 (318) 938 5402
www.ars.org

Canadian Rose Society
c/o Marie Farnady
504–334 Queen Mary Road
Kingston, Ontario K7M 7E7
www.canadianrosesociety.org

Heritage Rose Foundation
P.O. Box 831414
Richardson, TX 75083
USA

**National Rose Society of
Australia**
29 Columbia Crescent
Modbury North
SA 5092
Tel: +61 (0)8 8264 0084
www.rose.org.au

New Zealand Rose Society
P. O. Box 66
Bunnythorpe
Tel: +64 63 292 700
www.nzroses.org.nz

Royal National Rose Society
The Gardens of the Rose
Chiswell Green, St. Albans
Hertfordshire AL2 3NR
England
Tel: +44 (0)1727 850 461
www.rnrs.org

**The Rose Society of
Northern Ireland**
Mr Arthur Dixon (Secretary)
15 Lynden Gate
Ballyhannon Road
Portadown, BT63 5YH
Tel. +44 (0) 28 3833 4632
www.rosemerald.co.uk

**The Royal Horticultural
Society of Ireland (Rose
Group)**
Cabinteely House
The Park
Cabinteely
Co. Dublin
Tel: +353 (0)1 2353912
www.rhsi.ie

Société Française des Roses
Parc de la Tête d'Or
F-69459 Lyon
Tel: +33 (0)4 74 94 04 36

rose finder

| --- | --- | --- | --- | --- | --- |
'Climbing Mrs Sam McGredy'	Pergolas and arches	Eglantyne	Cutting (p102) Cottage gardens	Geoff Hamilton	Cottage gardens Cutting Scent Autumn and winter interest
'Climbing Old Blush'	Pergolas and arches Cottage gardens	'Empereur du Maroc'	Red roses (p21) Cutting Cottage gardens		
'Climbing Ophelia'	Pergolas and arches	Evelyn	Cottage gardens Cutting	Gertrude Jekyll	Cottage gardens Cutting Trailing over walls
'Climbing Souvenir de la Malmaison'	Pergolas and arches	Falstaff	Cottage gardens Cutting Red roses	'Gloire de Dijon'	Cottage gardens (p112) Pergolas and arches
'Complicata'	Poor soil conditions (p76) Winter interest Growing in small trees Hedging	'Fantin-Latour'	Balconies and roof gardens (p97) Cottage gardens Cutting	'Gloire des Mousseuses'	Cottage gardens Hedging Scent Cutting
'Comte de Chambord' ('Madame Knorr')	Cottage gardens Hedging Scent	'Felicia'	Hedges Cottage gardens Autumn and winter interest Scent	Golden Celebration	Special occasions (p124) Cottage gardens Cutting Scent
Congratulations	Special occasions (p127) Cutting Autumn and winter interest	'Félicité Parmentier'	Pergolas and arches	'Golden Showers'	Shaded positions (p28) Pergolas and arches
'Constance Spry'	Pergolas and arches Cottage gardens	'Félicité Perpétue'	Growing in trees (p49) Scent	Grace	Cottage gardens Cutting Scent
Cordelia	Pergolas and arches Cottage gardens	Fellowship ('Livin' Easy')	Contemporary gardens Pots and containers	Graham Thomas	Contemporary gardens (p104) Cottage gardens Cutting Scent
'Cornelia'	Pergolas and arches (p66) Trailing over walls Cottage gardens Cutting	'Ferdinand Pichard'	Curiosity (p121) Hedging Cottage gardens Cutting	'Guinée'	Red roses (p22) Pergolas and arches Scent
Crown Princess Margareta	Cottage gardens (p111) Cutting	Flower Carpet	Trailing over walls (p60) Ground cover Cottage gardens	Handel	Shaded positions (p31) Pergolas and arches Cutting
'Dainty Bess'	Small gardens (p92)	Fortune's Double Yellow (R. x odorata 'Pseudindica')	Pergolas and arches Security	'Henri Martin'	Poor soil conditions (p75) Hedging Security
'Danse du Feu'	Pergolas and arches Autumn interest	Fragrant Cloud	Scent (p14) Cutting	Heritage	Cottage gardens Cutting Hedging
'Debutante'	Pergolas and arches (p67) Trailing over walls	'François Juranville'	Pergolas and arches		
'Dioressence'	Contemporary gardens (p105) Pots and containers Cutting Scent	Freedom	Cutting	'Honorine de Brabant'	Cottage gardens Cutting Hedging
		'Fritz Nobis'	Autumn and winter interest (p118)		
'Doctor W. Van Fleet'	Growing in trees (p52–53) Cottage gardens	'Frühlingsgold'	Hedges (p34)	Iceberg	Small gardens Cottage gardens Cutting Autumn and winter interest
'Dortmund'	Red roses (p20) Pergolas and arches	'Général Schablikine'	Balconies and roof gardens (p96) Cottage gardens Cutting Pots and containers		
'Dream Girl'	Pergolas and arches Cottage gardens Scent			Ingrid Bergman	Cutting (p88) Red roses Autumn and winter interest
Dublin Bay	Pergolas and arches				
'Duchesse d'Angouléme'	Cottage gardens Cutting				

ROSE VARIETY	BEST FOR...	ROSE VARIETY	BEST FOR...	ROSE VARIETY	BEST FOR...
Intrigue	Red roses (p23) Pots and containers Cutting	'Leonardo da Vinci'	Cottage gardens Hedging	'Marian Finucane'	Pots and containers (p72) Cutting
Invincible	Cutting	'Leverkusen'	Pergolas and arches	'Meg'	Pergolas and arches Trailing over walls
'Ispahan'	Cottage gardens (p115) Hedging Cutting Scent	'Little White Pet'	Pots and containers (p69) Ground cover Autumn and winter interest Small gardens	'Mermaid'	Shaded positions (p27) Pergolas and arches Security
Jacqueline du Pré	Pots and containers (p68) Hedging Cutting	'Long John Silver'	Pergolas and arches Cutting Cottage gardens Trailing over walls	'Mevrouw Nathalie Nypels'	Small gardens (p93) Pots and containers Autumn and winter interest
Jacques Cartier ('Marchesa Boccella')	Cottage gardens Cutting Hedging Pots and containers	'Louis Van Tyle' ('Louis Van Till')	Cottage gardens Cutting	'Morning Jewel'	Contemporary gardens (p109)
James Galway	Thornless roses (p46) Cottage gardens Cutting Low walls	'Louis XIV'	Cutting Cottage gardens Red roses Scent	'Mrs Anthony Waterer'	Seaside locations (p82) Scent
'Jenny Duval'	Cottage gardens Hedging	'Louise Odier'	Cottage gardens Cutting	'Mrs John Laing'	Poor soil conditions (p78) Cutting
'Jubilee Celebration'	Cottage gardens Cutting	'Madame Alfred Carrière'	Shaded positions (p26) Pergolas and arches	'Mrs Oakley Fisher'	Small gardens Contemporary gardens
'Just Joey'	Cutting (p100)	'Madame Grégoire Staechelin' ('Spanish Beauty')	Pergolas and arches	'Nevada'	Hedges (p32) Contemporary gardens
Kent	Ground cover (p84) Pots and containers			'New Dawn'	Pergolas and arches Cottage gardens
Knock Out	Cutting Pots and containers Red roses Autumn and winter interest	'Madame Hardy'	Cottage gardens (p110) Hedging	Nostalgia	Cutting Contemporary gardens
		'Madame Isaac Pereire'	Scent (p18) Cottage gardens Cutting	'Nozomi'	Ground cover (p87) Cottage gardens
'Königin Von Dänemark' (Queen of Denmark)	Cottage gardens Cutting Hedging Scent	'Madame Louis Lévêque'	Balconies and roof gardens (p98) Pots and containers	Papa Meilland	Scent (p15) Cutting Red roses
'Korresia'	Small gardens (p90) Cutting Poor soil conditions	'Madame Pierre Oger'	Cottage garden Cutting	'Paul Transon'	Trailing over walls (p58) Pergolas and arches
'L.D. Braithwaite'	Red roses (p24) Cottage gardens Cutting	'Maigold'	Poor soil conditions (p74) Cutting Cottage gardens Pillars and archways Scent	'Paul's Himalayan Musk'	Growing in trees Pergolas (too big for arches)
'La Reine Victoria'	Cottage gardens Cutting	'Mammy Blue'	Cutting (p102) Contemporary gardens Scent	Peace ('Madame A. Meilland')	Cutting
'La Ville de Bruxelles'	Cutting	'Maréchal Niel'	Pergolas and arches	'Pegasus'	Cottage gardens Cutting
'Lamarque'	Pergolas and arches	Margaret Merril	Pots and containers (p70) Contemporary gardens Autumn and winter interest Scent	'Penelope'	Autumn and winter interest (p116) Hedging
'Leda'	Cottage gardens Cutting			'Perle d'Or'	Pergolas and arches Cottage gardens
'Le Rouge et le Noir'	Cutting Scent				

ROSE VARIETY	BEST FOR...
'Phyllis Bide'	*Trailing over walls (p61)* *Arches (not big enough for pergolas)* *Cottage gardens* *Small gardens*
'Pierre de Ronsard' (Eden Rose 88)	*Cutting (p103)* *Pergolas and arches*
'Président de Sèze'	*Hedging* *Cutting* *Cottage gardens*
'Prince Camille de Rohan'	*Cutting* *Cottage gardens*
'Pristine'	*Cutting* *Scent*
'Raubritter'	*Trailing over walls (p57)* *Ground cover*
'Reine des Violettes'	*Thornless roses (p44)* *Cutting* *Cottage gardens*
'Rhapsody in Blue'	*Scented (p19)* *Cutting* *Contemporary gardens* *Curiosity*
Rosa banksiae 'Lutea'	*Growing in trees (p50)* *Cottage gardens* *Pergolas and arches*
Rosa sericea subsp.omeiensis f. pteracantha	*Security (p38)* *Poor soil conditions*
Rosa x centifolia 'Cristata' ('Chapeau de Napoléon')	*Cottage gardens* *Scent* *Cutting*
Rosa x odorata 'Viridiflora'	*Curiosity (p123)* *Pergolas and arches* *Trailing over walls*
Rosa xanthina 'Canary Bird' ('Canary Bird')	*Hedging*
'Roseraie de l'Haÿ'	*Seaside locations (p83)* *Hedging* *Autumn and winter interest*
'Ruby Wedding'	*Special occasions (p127)* *Pots and containers* *Small gardens* *Cutting*
Saint Alban	*Cottage gardens* *Cutting* *Scent*

ROSE VARIETY	BEST FOR...
Saint Swithun	*Security (p40)* *Cottage gardens* *Cutting*
'Sally Holmes'	*Cottage gardens* *Contemporary gardens*
Savoy Hotel	*Cutting*
Scarborough Fair	*Cottage gardens* *Cutting* *Autumn and winter interest*
'Sénégal'	*Scented (p16)* *Pergolas and arches*
Sexy Rexy	*Pots and containers (p73)* *Cutting*
Sharifa Asma	*Cottage gardens* *Cutting* *Scent*
'Souvenir d'Adolphe Turc'	*Balconies and roof gardens (p99)* *Pots and containers*
'Souvenir de Georges Pernet'	*Security (p41)* *Cottage gardens* *Pergolas and arches* *Cutting*
'Souvenir de Saint Anne's'	*Cottage gardens* *Autumn and winter interest*
'Souvenir du Docteur Jamain'	*Scent (p17)* *Pergolas and arches* *Red roses*
Spirit of Freedom	*Contemporary gardens* *Trailing over walls*
'Stanwell Perpetual'	*Cottage gardens (p114)* *Hedging*
Super Dorothy ('Hedloro')	*Pergolas and arches* *Autumn and winter interest*
Super Excelsa ('Helexa')	*Pergolas and arches*
Sweet Juliet	*Contemporary gardens* *Cutting*
Teasing Georgia	*Cottage gardens* *Cutting* *Pergolas*
'Tess of the d'Urbervilles	*Cottage gardens* *Cutting* *Shaded positions*

ROSE VARIETY	BEST FOR...
The Alexandra Rose	*Cottage gardens* *Cutting* *Autumn and winter interest*
The Countryman	*Ground cover (p86)* *Cottage gardens* *Cutting*
The Dark Lady	*Cottage gardens* *Cutting* *Scent*
The Generous Gardener	*Pergolas and arches (p63)* *Cottage gardens* *Cutting*
The Mayflower	*Cottage gardens* *Cutting*
The Pilgrim	*Cottage gardens* *Cutting* *Scent*
The Shepherdess	*Cottage gardens* *Cutting* *Scent*
Trumpeter	*Pots and containers (p71)* *Small gardens*
'Tuscany Superb'	*Cottage gardens* *Hedging*
Valentine Heart	*Special occasions* *Cutting*
'Variegata di Bologna'	*Curiosity (p122)* *Cottage gardens*
'Veilchenblau'	*Thornless roses (p43)* *Pergolas and arches* *Scent*
Warm Wishes	*Special occasions (p125)*
'William Lobb'	*Cottage gardens* *Hedging* *Shaded positions*
William Shakespeare 2000	*Red roses (p25)* *Cottage gardens* *Cutting*
'Yesterday'	*Cutting* *Hedging* *Autumn and winter interest*
'Zéphirine Drouhin'	*Thornless roses (p47)* *Cottage gardens* *Cutting* *Scent*

index

acknowledgements

I'd like to thank my family who have been a great support. My mother and father Maura and Peter O'Neill, Carol and Robin Culleton, and Louise and James Duffy.

I owe a great debt of gratitude to Bill O'Sullivan who assisted me in the preparation of this book. A special thank you to Carmel Duignan whose diligence is always valued.

I want to acknowledge the tremendous support from my publishers. Thank you to Kyle Cathie for giving me the opportunity to make this book happen. Thanks also to the Kyle Cathie team, especially my editor Jennifer Wheatley who was such a pleasure to work with. I'd like to acknowledge the outstanding artistic skill that Sarah Cuttle has brought to this book with her amazing images of the roses. And Fran Rawlinson for designing the pages so beautifully. Thanks also to John Cooney, Hilary Mandleberg, Karen Collier, Vicki Murrell, Fiona St George, Ana Sampson and Sophie Flynn-Rogers who have all contributed with their time and expertise.

I am grateful for the support of many rose experts, especially to David Austin, Michael Mariott, Luke Stimpson, Sean McCann, David Kenny, Brian Hughes and Marie Hughes.

Of course, my experience of roses is very much a shared experience with so many gardening friends including Helen and Val Dillon, Frances and Iain MacDonald, Carl Dacus and Brian O'Donnell. Other good gardening friends who have shared their love of roses with me include Paul Gallagher, Thelma Mansfield, Stephen Smith, Corinne Hewat, Ricki Shannon, Janet Wynne, Anna Nolan, Nilla Martin, Angela Jupe, Noel Forde, Adelaide Monk, Suzanne McDougald, Alison Andrew and Peter Dobbin. There are many people in the Irish gardening trade who have given me great support, including Rachel Doyle, Thomas Quearney, Jim Clarke, Brian Wood and Breda Rosengrave.

Through the course of my work, I have made many good friends in the Irish media. They have all been of tremendous support to me and I'd like to say a special thank you to them all: Helen Rock, Charlie Wilkins, Philip Kampff, Tish Barry, Pat Kenny, Marian Richardson, Pat Costello, Marian Finucane, Derek Mooney, John O'Keeffe, Aoife Byrne, Cherrie McIlwaine, Julie Brown, Koraley Northen and Juliet Roberts.

I hope I'll be forgiven for names I may have omitted.

PICTURE CREDITS

All photography by Sarah Cuttle, except for the following:

Introduction
Page 8 (centre picture) Dermot O'Neill

Part 1: Best Roses for Special Purposes
Page 14 Jonathan Buckley
22 James Guilliam/Garden Picture Library (GPL)
23 David Askham/GPL
28 Zara McCalmont/GPL
34 Jerry Pavia/GPL
39 Jonathan Buckley
50 Neil Holmes/GPL
52–53 Marianne Majerus
60 Dermot O'Neill
64 Roger Phillips
72 Dermot O'Neill
74 Steffie Shields/Garden Matters
80 Marijke Heuff/GPL
84 David Askham/GPL
87 Roger Phillips
92 David Askham/GPL
93 Marianne Majerus
99 Roger Phillips
102 G Harper/GardenWorld Images
105 John & Irene Palmer/Garden Matters
113 Ellen Rooney/GPL
117 Didier Willery/GPL
120 Marily Young
125 Jonathan Buckley
126 Ron Evans/GPL
127 Marijke Heuff/GPL
127 John Feltwell/Garden Matters

Part 2: Directory
Page 129 Derek St Romaine Photography
131 (left) Bjorn Forsberg/GPL
132 (right) GardenWorld Images/Alamy
137 (left) Mark Bolton/GPL
138 (left) JS Sira/GPL
138 (right) as for page 129
140 (centre) James Guilliam/GPL
140 (right) Mark Bolton/GPL
141 Clay Perry
142 (far left) Roger Phillips
144 (left) John Glover/GPL
145 (left) John Glover/GPL
147 (left) Howard Rice/GPL
148 Roger Phillips
152 (top right) Clive Nichols/GPL
152 (bottom right) Lamontagne/GPL
154 (left) Roger Phillips
154 (right) Richard Bloom/GPL
155 (left) Howard Rice/GPL
155 (right) Roger Phillips
156 (left) Clive Nichols/GPL
158 (right) John Feltwell/Garden Matters
159 (bottom) Derek St Romaine Photography
161 (left) John Feltwell/Garden Matters
162 Roger Phillips
163 (top) Brian Carter/GPL
164 (left) Derek St Romaine Photography

Part 3: Rose Care
All photography by John Cooney except for:
Page 177 (left and right) Dermot O'Neill
180 Rex Butcher/GPL
181 (top left and top right) Dermot O'Neill
181 (top middle) Howard Rice/GPL
181 Andrew Darrington/Alamy